SACRED WISDOM

NATIVE AMERICAN WISDOM

A Spiritual Tradition At One With Nature

Edited by Alan Jacobs
Introduction by Dr Mick Gidley

WATKINS PUBLISHING
LONDON

This anthology of Native American Wisdom has been
selected by Alan Jacobs

This edition produced in 2008 for Sacred Wisdom,
an imprint of Watkins Publishing
Sixth Floor, Castle House, 75–76 Wells Street, London W1T 3QH
Distributed in the United States and Canada by
Sterling Publishing Co., Inc.
387 Park Avenue South, New York, NY 10016-8810

1 3 5 7 9 10 8 6 4 2

Designed in Great Britain by Jerry Goldie
Typeset in Great Britain by Dorchester Typesetting Group
Printed and bound in Malaysia for Imago

Library of Congress Cataloging-in-Publication data available

ISBN: 978-1-905857-86-9

www.watkinspublishing.co.uk

CONTENTS

Foreword *Alan Jacobs* v

Introduction *Mick Gidley* 1

Anishinaabeg	8	Lenni Lenape	61
Apache	10	Luiseño	63
Blackfoot	14	Navajo	68
Cherokee	15	Nez Percé	82
Cheyenne	20	Ojibwa	84
Chilliwack	22	Omaha	87
Chinook	29	Onondaga	90
Coast Salish	31	Osage	92
Cochiti	36	Paiute	102
Comanche	37	Papago	103
Creek	38	Passamaquoddy	107
Eskimo	42	Pawnee	108
Hopi	50	Pequot	119
Iroquois	51	Pima	121
Kiowa	54	Potawomi	125
Kwakiutl	56	Seneca	127

Shawnee	131	Suquamish	161
Sioux	133	Tewa	164
Dakota		Tlingit	166
(Santee Sioux)	135	Wabanaki	168
Lakota		Winnebago	169
(Teton Sioux)	143	Yuma	173
Oglala	149	Zuñi	174
Snehyttens	160		

Epilogue 181
Acknowledgements 186

FOREWORD

Native American Wisdom is multi-coloured, varied, and predominantly spiritual. It recognizes a Supreme Being, Guardian Spirits, Visionary Experience, Mythological Truth and Ceremonialism.

Many American Indian nations have created the beautiful strands of the essential wisdom, all with different hues and flavours yet with a common rhapsodic theme: the Sioux, Pawnee, Navajo, Apache, Iroquois, Cherokee, Cheyenne, Chinook, Ojibwa, Santee Dakota, Seneca, Comanche, Onondaga, Oglala Lakota, and many others. A single thread runs through this magnificent tapestry, that of a living spiritual world in another dimension of existence. There are gods and marvels, supernatural planes of being that make Nature sacred in every respect. Every single creature possesses a Soul.

The religion of the Native Americans includes prayer, ceremony, Sun Gods, Star Gods, Sky Beings and Ethereal Spirits – a veritable Celestial Sky held on high by a magnificent World Tree. They revere the brave Culture Heroes who deliver victory, institutions, rituals, guidance and inspiration to their fellow human beings. Women hold a high place in their divinatory structure and are respected for their love, motherhood, courage and wisdom. Dance, chant, music and elaborate decorative motifs (in their colourful carved wooden totem poles and woven rugs and shawls) play an important part in their rituals.

If we could enter the hearts and minds of Native Americans, before they were threatened by avaricious white settlers, we would see that they felt a great spirit world above them, wherever they went. The Earth was their mystic temple. Below the blue celestial sky, all their activities were a form of Nature worship. Glimpses of bright spirits flashed in the sunlight; they hovered, sending their messages to the brave and noble. The Supreme Being sets the rainbow in the clouds, which in due season water the land.

The wisdom of the Native Americans is profoundly holistic: an all-embracing pantheism pervades every aspect of their richly textured lives, which reflect their sound ecological and environmental beliefs. Their message has an important relevance at this time, when our planet is threatened by cataclysmic change brought about by man's greed and heedlessness.

In compiling this anthology I have come to love the soul of the Native American Indian. It is my earnest hope that this collection will enthuse and inspire all those who delve into the magic of its pages.

Alan Jacobs

INTRODUCTION

The native peoples of North America are extremely diverse. Their means of subsistence, their histories, their languages and their religions are marked by difference. The Hopis, living in stone town houses atop a series of high mesas in northern Arizona, are expert desert farmers. Their neighbours, the Navajos, by contrast, are a largely pastoral people, once semi-nomadic, who graze sheep and weave their wool into vibrant patterns. The Cherokees, originally settled in the moist valleys of the southern Appalachian mountains on the eastern seaboard, adapted so readily to aspects of Euro-American ways that by the beginning of the nineteenth century they were known as one of the 'Five Civilized Tribes' – but this did not prevent the forced removal of thousands of Cherokees across the Mississippi, along the infamous Trail of Tears, to Indian territory (later Oklahoma). Whether in the more arid environment of Oklahoma or among the hills of the Carolinas, they have struggled to survive as communities of farmers and by hunting for small game. The Kwakiutls, long-time inhabitants of villages along the coast of British Columbia at the northern end of Vancouver Island, look to the sea for their livelihood and to the surrounding rain forest for huge planks of timber for their homes. The Cheyennes, in their two branches, were traditionally nomadic peoples who camped in hide tipis as they hunted buffalo over a huge tract of the Great Plains; after their valiant resistance to white encroachment onto their lands during the last half of the nineteenth century, they were consigned to reservations in Montana and Oklahoma and constrained to small-scale farming and ranching.

These peoples, like many others who feature in *Native American Wisdom* (from which almost all the quotations in this Introduction are taken), are as disparate as the peoples of Europe, or more so. From the vantage of today, it is all too easy to forget that when Columbus arrived in the New World all of it was populated by an extraordinary array of peoples whose cultures had been created – and were continuing to evolve – in interaction with the specific geographies and climates, and with the other native cultures around them. Fully a third of the planet's root languages were spoken in the Americas, many of them deploying syntactical structures, sounds and meanings unique unto themselves. The scale of destruction in the hemisphere since has been catastrophic: vast areas of land have been totally denuded of their indigenous populations; entire nations, cultures and languages have been expunged, sometimes with barely a record of them ever having existed; and in the whole of the Americas there is now no nation state in which an indigenous people or language is dominant. Yet, despite the sheer scale of this devastation – and, importantly, despite the continuing frequent denigration of first nation peoples and their way of life – many indigenous languages do survive and, even where they are endangered now, a heritage of stories, sayings, songs, incantations and mythology has persisted. In North America, as the present volume testifies, new poems, tales, speeches and maxims have been – and are being – composed in English.

Despite the diversity among these peoples, a cardinal belief markedly held in common by all of them is reverence for the land. Jimme Derham, the present-day Cherokee artist and activist, has written: 'in the languages of my people ... there is a word for land: *eloheh*. This same word also means history, culture and religion. We cannot separate our place on Earth from our lives on the earth nor our vision nor our meaning as a people.' Towards the end of the nineteenth century, Ten Bears, the great Comanche chief, in his old age expressed his pride that he had been 'born upon the prairie' where 'there was nothing to break the light of the sun', and that he knew 'every stream and every wood between the Rio Grande and the Arkansas' rivers. And the Iroquois have a prayer, printed in full in this anthology, in which speakers 'return thanks to our mother, the earth', and then to 'the rivers and streams', to 'all herbs', to 'the corn, and to her sisters, the beans and squashes', and on through many of the other elements of the natural world. Everything is alive: not just the animal kingdom, but insects, trees and shrubs, the invisible wind, dust and stones.

Not surprisingly this veneration of the earth – which we can now see as in tune with modern ecological thought – is not only evident in the *content* of Indian verbal expressions, it is also part of their *form*. We can hardly help noticing that stories, songs and, especially, speeches brim with natural metaphors. Ohiyesa, a Sioux who was educated to become Charles A. Eastman, a medical doctor, author and an advocate of Indian interest at the turn of the twentieth century, remembered his uncle telling him that he 'ought to follow the example of the *shunktokecha*' (wolf): 'Even when he is surprised and runs for his life, he will pause to take one more look before he enters his final retreat. So you must take a second look at everything you see.' Chief Joseph of the Nez Percé, in one of his addresses to whites on behalf of those of his tribe exiled from their Oregon homeland at the end of the nineteenth century, said, 'You might as well expect the rivers to run backward as [expect] any man born free … to be contented [when] penned up.' The use of root metaphors – what Thomas Jefferson and other early commentators on native leaders' treaty speeches rightly considered 'natural' eloquence of Indian oratory – gives such expressions a sense of inevitability; everything they claim is, indeed, granted the authority of Nature itself. In another of his speeches, in a perfectly matter-of-fact manner, Joseph affirmed that 'the earth and myself are of one mind'.

Partly as a result of a century of Western movies, the prevalence of 'the Indian' as a stereotype – usually a be-feathered and war-painted Plains warrior, often cunning and cruel, sometimes drunk and stupid, and mostly silent except when whooping his war cries – means that it is often difficult for non-Indians to conceive of the variety and complexity of Native American cultures. It is truly hard to *hear* their expression. (Sometimes this is also a matter of translation: so much of the Indian material we encounter in English was collected by ethnologists of the late Victorian era who translated it into what now seems stilted prose that has squeezed out much of the vivacity and all of the frequent bawdiness of the originals.) But when prejudices are pushed aside, a different picture emerges. It is noticeable that many anthropologists' biog-raphical accounts of Indians emphasize what they see as the 'spirituality' of their subjects. A.C. Haddon, for example, a British founder of the discipline, titled one of his popular articles 'The Soul of the Red Man' (1914), and in it testified to 'the intensely religious nature' of the Indians he had encountered. This 'religious nature' is evident in the countless communal ceremonies referred to, however glancingly, in this book, whether performed by Hopis, Cherokees, Kwakiutls or Cheyennes.

Spirituality is also evident at a more individual level –

in the many references to the pursuit of 'dreams' and visionary states, often through fasting and solitude, sometimes through the powerful hallucinogen peyote. Such visions could give a person his or her name, mark the coming of age, or change the course of a life. Meditation of a less exalted kind and prayer – of which there are also numerous examples here – were the routine practices of most peoples. Whites have often considered Indians uncivilized 'savages', but Luther Standing Bear, who achieved considerable stature during the 1930s as a spokesperson for Native Americans, saw the irony of this judgement: 'I am going to venture that the man who sat on the ground in his tipi meditating on life and its meaning, accepting the kinship of all creatures and acknowledging unity with the universe of things, was infusing into his being the true essence of civilization.' The practice of 'civilization', in this sense, is also the attainment of wisdom.

This anthology of story, song and other forms, arranged alphabetically by the names of peoples or nations, unadulterated by any surrounding commentary, offers open and splendid access to this wisdom.

Mick Gidley
Emeritus Professor of American Literature and
Culture, University of Leeds

NATIVE
AMERICAN
WISDOM

ANISHINAABEG

When a young man reached manhood he selected the longest days in the year, which was generally late spring, and wandered away from the village into the lonely forest and there he would proceed to build a *wadiswan*, a nest, in some tree and he would lie down and commence his *giigwishimowin*, fast, which usually lasted from five to ten days without food or water. During the fast he had many dreams, and by those dreams the course of his future life was guided, both on the war path and in hunting.

Dream Poems

with a large bird

above me

i am walking

in the sky

i entrust

myself

to one wind

my feathers
sailing
on the breeze

honoring your brave men
like them
believing in myself

i am like the spirit
waiting
in my lodge
making me very old

APACHE

Prayer for Stalking Deer

This day

He who holds our roads,

Our sun father,

Has come out standing to his sacred place.

Now that he has passed us on our roads,

Here we pass you on your road.

Divine one,

The flesh of the white corn,

Prayer meal,

Shell,

Corn pollen,

Here I offer to you.

With your wisdom

Taking the prayer meal,

The shell,

The corn pollen,

This day,

My fathers,

My mothers,

In some little hollow,

In some low brush,

You will reveal yourselves to me.

Then with your flesh,

With your living waters,

May I sate myself.

In order that this may be

Here I offer you prayer meal.

Songs of the Masked Dancers

When the earth was made;

When the sky was made;

When my songs were first heard;

The holy mountain was standing toward me
    with life.

At the center of the sky, the holy boy walks four
    ways with life.

Just mine, my mountain became; standing
toward me with life.

Gan children became; standing toward me
with life.

When the sun goes down to the earth,

Where Mescal Mountain lies with its head
toward the sunrise,

Black spruce became; standing up with me.

Right at the center of the sky the holy boy with
life walks in four directions.

Lightning with life in four colors comes down
four times.

The place which is called black spot with life;

The place which is called blue spot with life;

The place which is called yellow spot with life;

The place which is called white spot with life.

Our Worship

We had no churches, no religious organizations, no sabbath day, no holidays, and yet we worshiped. Sometimes the whole tribe would assemble and sing and pray; sometimes a smaller number, perhaps only two or three. The songs had a few words, but were not formal. The singer would occasionally put in such words as he wished instead of the usual tone sound.

Sometimes we prayed in silence; sometimes each prayed aloud; sometimes an aged person prayed for all of us. At other times one would rise and speak to us of our duties to each other and to Usen. Our services were short.

Geronimo (Goyathlay), 1829–1909
Chiricahua Apache chief

Our Prayer

When a child my mother taught me the legends of our people; taught me of the sun and sky, the moon and stars, the clouds and storms. She also taught me to kneel and pray to Usen for strength, health, wisdom and protection. We never prayed against any person, but if we had aught against any individual we ourselves took vengeance. We were taught that Usen does not care for the petty quarrels of men.

Geronimo

BLACKFOOT

The Passage from Mother Earth to the Spirit World

What is life?

It is the flash of a firefly in the night.

It is the breath of a buffalo in the winter time.

It is the little shadow which runs across the grass

And loses itself in the Sunset.

Crowfoot, as he prepared for his journey
to the spirit world, 1890

The Sun God

We believe that the Sun God is all-powerful, for every Spring he makes the trees to bud and the grass to grow. We see these things with our own eyes, and therefore know that all life comes from him.

Anon

[The whites could not understand the deep spirituality of the Sun Dance of the Plains Indians, in which warriors underwent self-torture to strengthen their prayers. When this man spoke in 1910, the Sun Dance had been banned for a generation. Restrictions were lifted in the 1930s, and today there has been a revival of the old traditions.]

CHEROKEE

Formula for Obtaining Long Life

Now, then!

Ha, now thou hast come to listen, thou Long Human Being, thou art staying, thou Helper of human beings.

Thou never lettest go thy grasp from the soul.

Thou hast, as if it were, taken a firmer grasp upon
the soul.

I originated at the cataract, not so far away.

I will stretch out my hand to where thou art.

My soul has come to bathe itself in thy body.

The white foam would cling to my head as I walk
along the path of life, the white staff would
come into my extended hand.

The fire of the hearth will be left burning for me
incessantly.

The soul has been lifted up successively to the
seventh upper world.

Certainly I believe that ancient tribal cultures have
important lessons to teach the rest of the world about
the interconnectedness of all living things and the
simple fact that our very existence is dependent upon
the natural world we are rapidly destroying. Most
non-tribal societies have a hierarchical, segmented
world view. They appear not to understand or to
ignore the impact of their decisions on everything
around them ...

As native people approach the twenty-first century, we look into the faces of our youth and see ... hope. We would like to see that hope kept alive by doing everything possible to assure that our tribal communities continue to dig a way out of the devastation of the past 500 years. We look forward to the next 500 years as a time of renewal and revitalization for native people throughout North America.

Wilma Mankiller
First female Cherokee chief, 1980s

From the beginning there were drums, beating out world rhythm – the booming, never-failing tide on the beach; the four seasons, gliding smoothly, one from the other; when the birds come, when they go, the bear hibernating for his winter sleep. Unfathomable the why, yet all in perfect time.

Watch the heartbeat in your wrist – a precise pulsing beat of life's Drum – with loss of timing you are ill.

Jimalee Burton, 1974

Wit and Wisdom

You can learn a lot from Indians. They say you must never disagree with a man while you are facing him. Go around behind him and look the same way they do; look over his shoulder and get his viewpoint, then go back and face him, and you will have a different idea.

It's great to be great, but it's greater to be human.

Everything worthwhile is a good idea, but did you ever notice there is more bad ideas that will work than there is good ones?

Be sure you are right and then go ahead, but don't arbitrate.

Whether your parents are good or bad, that's not your business, but stick with 'em when they are in trouble.

No man is great if he thinks he is.

People love high ideals, but they got to be about 33 percent plausible.

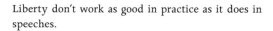

Liberty don't work as good in practice as it does in speeches.

A fool that knows he is a fool, is one that knows he don't know all about anything. But the fool that don't know he is a fool, is the one that thinks he knows all about anything.

There is nothing as easy as denouncing. It don't take much to see that something is wrong, but it does take some eyesight to see what will put it right again.

A remark generally hurts in proportion to its truth.

Don't just grab at the first thing that comes along. Have an idea in your head and be willing to wait for it. Know when to refuse something that won't get you anywhere. Struggle along for years, you got to wait for a thing till it is ripe; don't just pump into things just because somebody offers it to you. Look and see if it's going to lead you anywhere.

Lead your life so you wouldn't be ashamed to sell the family parrot to the town gossip.

Will Rogers
Philosopher/comedian (half Cherokee)

CHEYENNE

Scout's Song

Take courage;

Do not be frightened;

Follow where you see me riding my white
horse.

Sitting Bull's Song

Pretty bird, you saw me and took pity on me;

You wished me to survive among the people.

O Bird People, from this day always you shall be
my relatives!

The Raven Says

Our father above, I have seen.

The raven says, 'There is going to be another
judgement day.'

Song of the Ghost Dance

The crow

I saw him when he flew down

To the earth

He has renewed our life

He has taken pity on us

In Battle

The idea of full dress in preparation for a battle comes not from belief that it will add to the fighting ability. The preparation is for death, in case that should be the result of the conflict. Every Indian wants to look his best when he goes to meet the great Spirit, so the dressing up is done whether an imminent danger is an oncoming battle or a sickness or injury at times of peace.

Wooden Leg, late 19th century

Our Earth

The old Indian teaching was that it is wrong to tear loose from its place on the earth anything that may be growing there. It may be cut off, but it should not be uprooted. The trees and the grass have spirits. Whenever one of such growths may be destroyed by some good Indian, his act is done in sadness and with a prayer for forgiveness because of his necessities ...

Wooden Leg

CHILLIWACK

The Beginning of the World

Long, long ago,

Before anything was,

Saving only the heavens,

From the seat of his golden throne,

The Sun-god looked out on the Moon-goddess,

And found her beautiful.

Hour after hour,

With hopeless love,

He watched the spot where, at evening,

She would sometimes come out to
  wander

Through her silver garden

In the cool of the dusk.

Far he sent his gaze across the heavens

Until the time came, one day,

When she returned his look of love

And she, too, sat lonely,

Turning eyes of wistful longing

Toward her distant lover.

Then their thoughts of love and
  longing,

Seeking each other,

Met halfway,

Mingled,

Hung suspended in space ...

Thus: the beginning of the world.

Sat they long in loneliness,

The great void of eternal space

Closing in upon them.

Despair hung heavy in their hearts.

Gone was the splendor of the golden
 throne;

Gone was the beauty of the silver
 garden;

Their souls burned with a white flame
 of longing.

Up leaped the Sun-god,

Chanting his love song,

The words of his love thoughts:

> My heart wings its way to you,
>
> O daughter of the Moon!
>
> My heart wings its way to you,
>
> Where you stand,

In your silver garden,

Your white face turned toward me.

You will receive a gift,

O daughter of the Moon!

A gift of my great love

For you only;

You will receive a gift of my love

This day, ere the dusk falls.

Then,

From his place at the gate of the Sun,

He, the Sun-god,

Raised his arm high

And cast his message

Far into the sky.

Swift it flew,

Following an unerring course

Toward the distant garden

Where sat the Moon-goddess.

But what of the message?

Alas! It wavers in its flight;

Drops;

Falls on the embryo world;

Thus: the land.

Far across the heavens,

In her silver garden,

The Moon-goddess wept bitterly.

A tear was borne by the wind;

Fell on the half-formed world;

Thus: the water.

There from the love thoughts,

Longings and love words,

Sprang beautiful trees and flowers.

Little streams gurgled through the
forests;

Leaping waterfalls foamed;

Great rivers flowed to the sea;

Fish abounded;

Buffalo roamed the plains

And through the wood-paths

Sped all the wild things

Of a new world.

The Sun-god left the seat of his golden
    throne;

Swung wide that gate of the Sun!

A ringing shout cleft the heavens!

He seized his knife

And with swift slashes,

Tore a strip of bark

From a great tree.

Still he chanted his songs

Of love and longing,

As he wrote on the birch bark

In the speech of springtime,

The language of lovers.

The Moon-goddess,

From her silver garden,

Heard the cry;

Stood,

And answered.

He of the Sun,

She of the Moon,

Stood they

With arms outstretched

A moment

Silent.

Then, in the first shadow of evenfall,

They leaped into space;

Came to rest

On the new world of their love;

Thus: the first man and woman.

Khalserten Sepass, or 'Lord of the waterfalls',
c.1840–1945

[This Chilliwack chief decided to make public the ancient secret songs that belonged to him before they became lost forever. From 1911 to 1915 he recited 'The Songs of Y-Ail-Myhth,' a cycle of sixteen songs sacred to his people, to Eloise Street, who, as editor of *Indian Time*, published them much later. This song is the first of the series.]

CHINOOK

Teach Us, and Show Us the Way

Teach us, and show us the Way.

We call upon the earth, our planet home, with its beautiful depths and soaring heights, its vitality and abundance of life, and together we ask that it

Teach us, and show us the Way.

We call upon the mountains, the Cascades and the Olympics, the high green valleys and meadows filled with wild flowers, the snows that never melt, the summits of intense silence, and we ask that they

Teach us, and show us the Way.

We call upon the waters that rim the earth, horizon to horizon, that flow in our rivers and streams, that fall upon our gardens and fields and we ask that they

Teach us, and show us the Way.

We call upon the land which grows our food, the nurturing soil, the fertile fields, the abundant gardens and orchards, and we ask that they

Teach us, and show us the Way.

We call upon the forests, the great trees reaching strongly to the sky with earth in their roots and the heavens in their branches, the fir and the pine and the cedar, and we ask them to

Teach us, and show us the Way.

We call upon the creatures of the fields and forests and the seas, our brothers and sisters the wolves and deer, the eagle and dove, the great whales and the dolphin, the beautiful Orca and salmon who share our Northwest home, and we ask them to

Teach us, and show us the Way.

We call upon all those who have lived on this earth, our ancestors and our friends, who dreamed the best for future generations, and upon whose lives our lives are built, and with thanksgiving, we call upon them to

Teach us, and show us the Way.

And lastly, we call upon all that we hold most
sacred, the presence and power of the Great Spirit
of love and truth which flows through all the
Universe, to be with us to

Teach us, and show us the Way.

Anon, 18th century

COAST SALISH

A Masked Event for Comedian and Audience

1. A comedian's mask is painted red on one
   side, black on the other; the mouth is
   twisted, the hair in disarray. For a costume
   he wears a blanket or a strip of fur which
   leaves his right hand free. He dances along
   with the other performers, often dances out-
   of-time to attract attention, and repeatedly
   annoys the dancers by quizzically
   scrutinizing theirs masks, poking at their
   eyes, looking at their noses, picking their
   teeth, etc. Sometimes the dancers whip the
   comedian vigorously with cedar boughs to
   drive him away, keeping time with the

drums as they do so. When not annoying
the dancers, the comedian goes around the
room pretending to take lice from the
singers' hair. He sometimes goes to a very
old woman or a very pretty girl to do this,
using it as a pretext to caress her.

2. The audience refrains from laughing.

Our Earth

Everything on the earth has a purpose,

Every disease and herb to cure it,

And every person a mission.

This is the Indian theory of existence.

Mourning Dove
(Christine Quintasket), 1888–1936

On Children

Children were encouraged to develop strict discipline
and a high regard for sharing. When a girl picked her
first berries and dug her first roots, they were given
away to an elder so she would share her future

success. When a child carried water for the home, an elder would give compliments, pretending to taste meat in water carried by a boy or berries in that of a girl. The child was encouraged not to be lazy and to grow straight like a sapling.

Mourning Dove

On Marriage

For an important marriage the chief presided, aided by his wife. He passed a pipe around the room so each could share a smoke in common. In this way families were publicly united to banish any past or future disagreements and thus stood as 'one united'. The chief then gave the couple an oration of his advice, pointing out the good characteristics of each, and then offered his congratulations to them for a happy future.

Mourning Dove

On Lost Spirits

It was supposed that lost spirits were roving about everywhere in the invisible air, waiting for children to find them if they searched long and patiently enough ... [The spirit] sang its spiritual song for the child to memorize and use when calling upon the spirit guardian as an adult.

Mourning Dove

My Heart Soars

The beauty of the trees,

the softness of the air,

the fragrance of the grass

speaks to me.

The summit of the mountain,

the thunder of the sky,

the rhythm of the sea,

speaks to me.

The faintness of the stars,

the freshness of the morning,

the dewdrop of the flower,

speaks to me.

The strength of fire,

the taste of salmon,

the trail of the sun,

And the life that never goes away,

they speak to me.

And my heart soars.

Chief Dan George

COCHITI

The Origin of Death

They were coming up from Shipap. One of their children became sick and they did not know what was the trouble with him. They had never seen sickness before. They said to the Shkoyo [curing society] chief, 'Perhaps our Mother in Shipap will help us. Go back and ask her to take away this trouble.' He went back to our Mother and she said to him, 'The child is dead. If your people did not die, the world would fill up and there would be no place for you to live. When you die, you will come back to Shipap to live with me. Keep on traveling and do not be troubled when your people die.'

He returned to his people and told them what our Mother had said. In those days they treated one another as brothers, all the Indians of all the Pueblos. They planted corn with the digging stick and they were never tired; they dug trenches to irrigate their fields. The corn ripened in one day. When they came to Frijoles they separated, and the different pueblos went their own ways.

From Ruth Benedict, *Tales of the Cochiti Indians*

[The counsel of the Mother who resides at Shipap – the place of emergence and the realm of the dead – is quite in keeping with Pueblo philosophy. Excessive mourning is harmful and will interfere with the welfare not only of the living, but also of the dead. In another Cochiti story we hear that a child that had died could not find rest because her mother did not stop crying.]

COMANCHE

Song of the Ghost Dance

The sun's beams are running out

The sun's beams are running out

The sun's yellow rays are running out

The sun's yellow rays are running out

We shall live again

We shall live again

I Lived Happily

I was born upon the prairie, where the wind blew free, and there was nothing to break the light of the sun. I was born where there were no enclosures, and where everything drew a free breath … I know every stream and every wood between the Rio Grande and the Arkansas. I have hunted and lived over that country. I lived like my fathers before me, and like them, I lived happily.

Ten Bears (Parra-wa-samem), late 19th century
Yamparethka Comanche chief

CREEK

Poetry of Alex Posey, 19th century:

Nature's Blessings

'Tis mine to be in love with life,

And mine to hear the robins sing;

'Tis mine to live apart from strife,

And kneel to flowers blossoming –

To all things fair,

As at a shine —

To drink the air

As I would wine.

To Love I've built a temple here,

Beneath the boughs of oak and
pine,

Beside a spring that all the year

Tells of a harmony divine.

I own no creeds

Sweet Love beside —

My spirit's needs

Are satisfied.

A Vision Of June

At last, my white Narcissus is in bloom;

Each blossom sheds a wonderful
fragrance. Lo!

From over bleak December's waste of snow,

In summer garments, lightly thro' the gloom,

Comes June to claim the truant in my room;

> With her the airs of sunny meadows
> come,

> And in the apple boughs I hear the hum

Of bees; in all the valleys, brooks resume,

'Twixt greening banks, their murmurous
melody;

The sunlight bursts in splendour in the blue,

> And soon the narrow walls confining me

Recede into the distance from my view;

> My spirit in the summer's largeness
> grows,

> And every thorn is hidden by the rose.

A Simile

> Like bits of broken glass,
>
> Chance scatters in the sun,
>
> Our deeds reflect the light
>
> We carry on the world.

A Reverie

The sky bends over in a sweet
Forgiveness; earth is filled with light;
And mellow autumn hues, soft winds
That croon of summer lands; and thro'
The brooding stillness comes a strain
Of music, and, as leaves are swept
Upon the river's tide away,
My thoughts drift off and on to God.

The Poet's Song

The poet sings but fragments of
A high-born melody –
A few stray notes and castaways
Of perfect harmony
That come to him like murmurs from
The sea of mystery.

Assured

Be it dark; be it bright;

   Be it pain; be it rest;

Be it wrong; be it right –

   It must be for the best.

Some good must somewhere wait,

   And sometime joy and pain

Must cease to alternate,

   Or else we live in vain.

ESKIMO

Spring Song, Fragment

Glorious it is

To see young women

Gathering in little groups

And paying visits in the houses –

Then all at once the men

Do so want to be manly ...

... Glorious it is

To see long haired winter caribou

Returning to the forests ...

... While the herd follows the ebb-mark
of the sea

With a storm of clattering hooves.

Glorious it is

When wandering time is come.

From Knud Rasmussen,
Intellectual Culture of the Iglulik Eskimos

Utitiáq's Song

Aja, I am joyful; this is good!

Aja, there is nothing but ice around me, that is
good!

Aja, I am joyful, this is good!

My country is nothing but slush, that is good!

Aja, I am joyful, this is good!

Aja, when, indeed, will this end? This is good!

I am tired of watching and waking, this is good!

Cumberland Sound Eskimo
From Franz Boas, *Eskimo Tales and Songs*

[This song was composed, says Boas, by a young man named Utitiáq, who went adrift on the ice when sealing, and did not reach the shore until after a week of hardships and privations.]

The Rainbow

Peace after the storms of war and suffering, God's covenant with mankind through His Prophets, and the union of all the colors of the races of mankind in pleasing harmony ... – this is the symbol of the rainbow.

Seal hunter, early 20th century
From William Willoya, *Warriors of the Rainbow*

Two Songs From Eskimo Point

1   I recall something.

I recall the words of a stranger
    about forever.

A person came down from the sky,
    telling them not to be afraid;
    they would be hearing
    about life, spiritual life, soul.
A baby will be born.

2   How am I going to sing? The lead dog
    just gets angry in the deep snow.
In the deep snow I have to run
    to follow the tracks.

I want to get closer to you.

Improvised Song of Joy

Ajaja – aja – jaja,

The lands around my dwelling

Are more beautiful

From the day

When it is given me to see

Faces I have never seen before.

All is more beautiful,

All is more beautiful,

And life is thankfulness.

These guests of mine

Make my house grand,

Ajaja – aja – jaja.

From Knud Rasmussen,
Intellectual Culture of the Iglulik Eskimos

[The old woman Takomaq, who was about to serve a meal she had prepared for Rasmussen and his companion, was so pleased at the sight of the tea he contributed that she at once joyfully improvised the above song.]

The Land of Heaven

Heaven is a great land. In that land there are many holes. These holes we call stars. In the land of heaven lives Pana [the Woman-up-there]. There is a mighty spirit, and the *angatkut* hold that it is a woman. To her pass the souls of the dead. And sometimes, when many die, there are many people up there. When anything is spilt up there, it pours out through the stars and becomes rain or snow. The souls of the dead are reborn in the dwellings of Pana and brought down to earth again by the moon. When the moon is absent, and cannot be seen in the sky, it is because it is busy helping Pana by bringing souls to earth. Some become human beings once more, others become animals, all manner of beasts. And so life goes on without end.

Caribou Eskimo

A Woman's First Sewing after a Mourning

Whose claws have I for pinch-fingers?

The bat's claws I have for pinch-fingers,

On account of my housewife work.

Whose claws have I for pinch-fingers?

The crab's claws I have for pinch-fingers,

On account of my housewife work.

From A. Grove Day, The Sky Clears:
Poetry of the American Indians

[This magic formula was used by a woman the first time she began to sew again after a period of mourning. The idea is familiar as compulsive magic; the primitive mind believes that if you say you have special powers, these powers will be granted to you.]

Walrus Hunting

The walrus, I harpoon it,

Stroking its cheek.

You have become quiet and meek.

The walrus, I harpoon it,

Patting its tusks.

You have become quiet and meek.

From A. Grove Day, The Sky Clears

[Incantations to insure good hunting were common among all natives from the Artic to the Equator. In this example

the hunter hoped the charm would subdue the fierceness
of the walrus, so that it might be easily harpooned when
the close fighting began.]

The Kayak Paddler's Joy at the Weather

When I'm out of the house in the open,

I feel joy.

When I get out on the sea on haphazard,

I feel joy.

If it is really fine weather,

I feel joy.

If the sky really clears nicely,

I feel joy.

May it continue thus

for the good of my sealing!

May it continue thus

for the good of my hunting!

May it continue thus

for the good of my singing-match!

May it continue thus

for the good of my drum-song!

HOPI

Korosta Katzina Song
(Corn Blessing Song)

Yellow butterflies,

Over the blossoming virgin corn,

With pollen-painted faces

Chase one another in brilliant throng.

Blue butterflies,

Over the blossoming virgin beans,

With pollen-painted faces

Chase one another in brilliant streams.

Over the blossoming corn,

Over the virgin corn,

Wild bees hum;

Over the blossoming beans,

Over the virgin beans,

Wild bees hum.

Over your field of growing corn

    All day shall hang the thunder-cloud;

Over your field of growing corn

    All day shall come the rushing rain.

IROQUOIS

At the Wood's Edge

Now today I have been greatly startled by your voice coming through the forest to this opening. You have come with troubled mind through all obstacles. You kept seeing the places where they met on whom we depended, my offspring. How then can your mind be at ease?

You kept seeing the footmarks of our forefathers; and all but perceptible is the smoke where they used to smoke the pipe together. Can then your mind be at ease when you are weeping on your way?

Great thanks now, therefore, that you have safely arrived. Now, then, let us smoke the pipe together. Because all around are hostile agencies which are each thinking, 'I will frustrate their purpose.' Here thorny ways, and here falling trees, and here wild beasts lying in ambush. Either by these you might have perished, my offspring, or by the uplifted hatchet in the dark outside the house. Every day these are wasting us; or deadly invisible disease might have destroyed you, my offspring.

Great thanks now, therefore, that in safety you have come through the forest.

Death of a Son

My son, listen once more to the words of your mother. You were brought into life with her pains. You were nourished with her life. She has attempted to be faithful in raising you up. When you were young she loved you as her life. Your presence has been a source of great joy to her. Upon you she depended for support and comfort in her declining days. She had always expected to gain the end of the path of life before you. But you have outstripped her, and gone before her. Our great and wise creator has ordered it thus. By his will I am left to taste more of the miseries of this world. Your friends and relatives have gathered about your body, to look upon you for the last time. They mourn, as with one mind, your departure from among us. We, too, have but a few

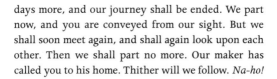

days more, and our journey shall be ended. We part now, and you are conveyed from our sight. But we shall soon meet again, and shall again look upon each other. Then we shall part no more. Our maker has called you to his home. Thither will we follow. *Na-ho!*

Prayer

We return thanks to our mother, the earth, which sustains us. We return thanks to the rivers and streams, which supply us with water. We return thanks to all herbs, which furnish medicines for the cure of our diseases. We return thanks to the corn, and to her sisters, the beans and squashes, which give us life. We return thanks to the bushes and trees, which provide us with fruit. We return thanks to the wind, which, moving the air, has banished diseases. We return thanks to the moon and stars, which have given to us their light when the sun was gone. We return thanks to our grandfather Hé-no, that he has protected his grandchildren from witches and reptiles, and has given to us his rain, We return thanks to the sun, that he has looked upon the earth with a beneficent eye. Lastly, we return thanks to the Great Spirit, in whom is embodied all goodness, and who directs all things for the good of his children.

Dream Events

After having a dream, let someone else guess what it was. Then have everyone act it out together.

Have participants run around the center of a village, acting out their dreams and demanding that others guess and satisfy them.

KIOWA

The Word

A word has power in and of itself. It comes from nothing into sound and meaning; it gives origin to all things. By means of words can a man deal with the world on equal terms. And the word is sacred. A man's name is his own; he can keep it or give it away as he likes. Until recent times, the Kiowas would not speak the name of a dead man. To do so would have been disrespectful and dishonest. The dead take their names with them out of the world.

On Prayer

The Peyote Man prays

to an unknown mystery

he has no name for it

    but life

The Peyote Man prays

to a great light

to the great light

to understand the light

    within himself

Fróm Willard Rhodes,
Music of the American Indian

Warpath Song

I ran to the brook to do my hair.

I painted my face with colors of the evening
skies.

My aunt chose a bright blue shawl for me,
blue as the sky.

But then we heard the cry that meant

darkness to all my people.

I ran back to my tent.

I washed off all the paint

with my tears.

Trans. Maurice Boyd

KWAKIUTL

Song

Do not let our chief rise too high

Do not let him destroy too much property

else we shall be made like broken pieces of
  copper by the

  great breaker of coppers

  the great splitter of coppers

  the great chief who throws coppers into the
  water

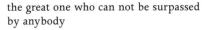

the great one who can not be surpassed
by anybody

the one surmounting all the chiefs

Shaman's Song

I have been told to continue to heal him, by the
good supernatural power.

I have been told to keep on putting the hemlock
ring over him, by the Shaman-of-the-sea, the
good supernatural power.

I have been told to put back into our friend his
soul, by the good supernatural power.

I have been told to give him long life, by the
Long-Life-Giver-of-the-Sea, the Chief-of-High-
Water, the good supernatural power.

'Put our friend through the ring.' Thus I was told
by the supernatural power.

'Spray our friend!' Thus I was told by the
supernatural power.

'Heal our friend!' Thus I was told by the
supernatural power.

'Take out [the weakness] of our friend!'

Thus I was told by the supernatural power.

I come and bring back this means of bringing to
life our friend, Supernatural Power.

Come now means-of-bringing-to-life of our
Shaman-of-the-Sea of our friend, Supernatural
Power.

Make well all over our friend, that no ill may
befall our poor friend, supernatural power.

Now you will protect our poor friend, that he may
walk safely, Supernatural Power.

Now, Supernatural Power, cure our poor friend
and make him well again, O Great Real
Supernatural Power, Supernatural Power.

Now, Supernatural Power, turn him the right way
and make well our friend here, you, Great Real
Supernatural Power, Healer-of-the-Sea.

Now take this, Supernatural Power, Spirit-of-the-
Fire, this which will cure our friend here, you,
Great Real Supernatural Power, Fire-Spirit-
Woman.

And do protect our friend, you, Fire-Spirit-
Woman, Great Supernatural Power.

Songs of the Sun and Moon

The first man holds it in his hands,
He holds the sun in his hands.
In the center of the sky, he holds it in his hands.
As he holds it in his hands, it starts upward.

The first woman holds it in her hands,
She holds the moon in her hands.
In the center of the sky, she holds it in her hands.
As she holds it in her hands, it starts upward.

The first man holds it in his hands,
He holds the sun in his hands.
In the center of the sky, he holds it in his hands.
As he holds it in his hands, it starts downward.

The first woman holds it in her hands,
She holds the sun in her hands.
In the center of the sky, she holds it in her hands.
As she holds it in her hands, it starts downward.

There Are No People Song

You say there were no people

    Smoke was spreading [over the earth].

You say there were no people.

    Smoke was spreading.

First Man was the very first to emerge, they say,

    Smoke was spreading.

He brought with him the various robes and
precious things, they say,

    Smoke was spreading.

He brought with him the white corn and the
yellow corn, they say,

    Smoke was spreading.

He brought with him the various animals and
the growing things, they say,

    Smoke was spreading.

You say there were no people.

    Smoke was spreading.

First Woman was the very first to emerge,
  they say,

    Smoke was spreading.

On Law

'It is a strict law that bids us dance. It is a strict law that bids us distribute our property among our friends and neighbors.'

Anon, c.1886

LENNI LENAPE

Creation Hymn

in the beginning of the world

    all men had knowledge cheerfully

    all had leisure

    all thoughts were pleasant

at that time all creatures were friends

wide waters rushing

wide to the hills

everywhere spreading

waters devouring

men and all creatures on the flood of
the waters

when the daughter of the spirit came to
help

all then joined together

all saying

Come help

in other years all traveled

over the waters of the hard stony sea

all were peaceful long ago

large and long was the east land

rich and good

shall we be free and happy then

at the new land?

we want rest in peace and wisdom

Adapted from E.G. Squier, '… translation of the
Walum-Olum, or Bark Record of the Lenni Lenape',
first printed in *The American Whig Review*, 1849

LUISEÑO

The Creation Myth

In the beginning all was empty space. Ké-vish-a-tak-vish was the only being. This period was called *Om-ai-ya-mai*, signifying emptiness, nobody there. Then came the time called *Ha-ruh-rug*, upheaval, things coming into shape. Then a time called *Chu-tu-tai*, the falling of things downward, and after this, *Yu-vai-to-vai*, things working in darkness without the light of sun or moon. Then came the period *Tul-mul Pu-shim*, signifying that deep down in the heart of the earth things were working together.

Then came *Why-yai Pee-vai*, a gray glimmering like the whiteness of hoar frost; and then, *Mit' ai Kwai-rai*, the dimness of twilight. Then came a period of cessation, *Na-kai Ho-wai-yai*, meaning things at standstill. Then Ké-vish-a-tak-vish made a man, Tuk-mit, the sky, and a woman, To-mai-yo-vit, the Earth. There was no light, but in the darkness these two became conscious of each other.

'Who are you?,' asked the man.

'I am Tu-mai-yo-vit. I am stretched, I am extended. Shake, I resound. I am diminished, I am earthquake. I revolve, I roll, I disappear. And who are you?'

'I am Ké-vish-a-tak-vish. I am night. I am inverted. I cover, I rise. I devour, I drain [by death]. I seize, I send away the souls of men. I cut, I sever life.'

'Then you are my brother.'

'Then you are my sister.'

And by her brother, the Sky, the Earth conceived and became the mother of all things.

From Constance G. Du Bois,
'Mythology of the Mission Indians', *Journal of the American Folklore Society*, vol. 19

[This myth has resonances from The Creation Hymns of the Rig Veda.]

A Speech to the Dead

Now this day you have ceased to see daylight.

Think only of what is good.

Do not think of anything uselessly.

You must think all the time of what is good.

You will go and live with our nephew.

And do not think evil towards these your relatives.

When you start to leave them this day you must not think backwards of them with regret.

And do not think of looking back at them.

And do not feel badly because you have lost sight of this daylight.

This does not happen today to you alone, so that you thus be alone when you die.

Bless the people so that they may not be sick.

This is what you will do.

You must merely bless them so that they may live as mortals here.

You must always think kindly.

Today is the last time I shall speak to you.

Now I shall seize speaking to you, my relative.

Chief Fox

Songs of the Seasons

I
The ant has his season;

he has opened his house.

When the days grow warm he comes out.

The spider has her house and her hill.

The butterfly has her enclosure.

The chipmunk and squirrel have their
hollowed logs for acorns.

It is time for the eagle to take off.

It will soon be time for the acorns to fall from
the trees.

II
In the north the bison have their
breeding grounds,

and the elk drops her young.

    In the east the mountain sheep

and the horn toad have their young.

    In the south other animals give birth.

In the west the ocean is heaving,

    tossing its waves back and forth.

Here, at this place, the deer sheds his hair

    and the acorns grow fat.

The sky sheds, changing color,

    white clouds swept away.

III

The Milky Way lies stretched out on its back,

    making a humming sound.

From the door of my house I recognize

    in the distance Nahut, the stick used

    to beat Coyote, and Kashlapish,

    the ringing stones. I look up.

Look: Antares is rising,

Altair is rising. The Milky Way,

Venus is rising.

From Constance G. Du Bois,
The Religion of the Luiseño Indians

NAVAJO

Songs in the Garden of the House God

Truly in the east

The white bean

And the green corn-plant

Are tied with the white lightning.

Listen! Rain approaches!

The voice of the bluebird is heard.

Truly in the east

The white bean

And the great squash

Are tied with the rainbow.

Listen! Rain approaches!

The voice of the bluebird is heard.

From the top of the great corn-plant the water
  gurgles, I hear it;

Around the roots the water foams, I hear it;

Around the roots of the plants it foams, I hear it;

From their tops the water foams, I hear it.

The corn grows up. The waters of the dark
  clouds drop, drop.

The rain descends. The waters from the corn
  leaves drop, drop.

The rain descends. The waters from the plants
  drop, drop.

The corn grows up. The waters of the dark
  mists drop, drop.

Shall I cull this fruit of the great corn-plant?

Shall you break it? Shall I break it?

Shall I break it? Shall you break it?

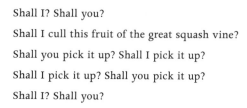

Shall I? Shall you?

Shall I cull this fruit of the great squash vine?

Shall you pick it up? Shall I pick it up?

Shall I pick it up? Shall you pick it up?

Shall I? Shall you?

First Song of the Thunder

Thonah! Thonah!

There is a voice above,

The voice of the thunder.

Within the dark cloud,

Again and again it sounds,

Thonah! Thonah!

Thonah! Thonah!

There is a voice below,

The voice of the grasshopper.

Among the plants,

Again and again it sounds,

Thonah! Thonah!

Twelfth Song of the Thunder

The voice that beautifies the land!

The voice above,

The voice of the thunder,

Within the dark cloud

Again and again it sounds,

The voice that beautifies the land.

The voice that beautifies the land!

The voice below:

The voice of the grasshopper.

Among the plants

Again and again it sounds,

The voice that beautifies the land.

Two thunder songs from the Mountain Chant

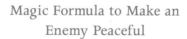

Magic Formula to Make an Enemy Peaceful

Put your feet down with pollen.

Put your hands down with pollen.

Put your head down with pollen.

Then your feet are pollen;

Your hands are pollen;

You body is pollen;

Your mind is pollen;

Your voice is pollen.

The trail is beautiful.

Be still.

In Beauty May I Walk

In beauty may I walk.

All day long may I walk.

Through the returning seasons
  may I walk ...

On the trail marked with pollen
  may I walk.

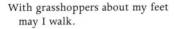

With grasshoppers about my feet
  may I walk.

With dew about my feet may I walk.

With beauty may I walk.

With beauty before me, may I walk.

With beauty behind me, may I walk.

With beauty above me, may I walk.

With beauty below me, may I walk.

With beauty all around me, may I walk.

In old age wandering on a trail of beauty,

Lively, may I walk.

In old age wandering on a trail of beauty,

Living again, may I walk.

It is finished in beauty.

It is finished in beauty.

From the Nightway Chant

Nature

Know things in nature
are like a person.
Talk to tornados;
talk to the thunder.
They are your friends
and will protect you.

Anon

I Walk in Beauty

O, you who live in Tsegíhi,

in the house made of dawn,

in the house made of evening twilight,

in the house made of dark cloud,

in the house of male rain,

in the house made of female rain, in the house
made of pollen,

in the house made of grasshoppers,

where dark mists drop over the door

to which the path on the rainbow stretches,

where the zigzag lightning stands high,

where the male rain stands high,

O, male god,

with your shoes of dark cloud, come to us,

with your leggings of dark cloud, come to us,

with your shirt of dark cloud, come to us,

with your headdress of dark cloud, come to us,

With your mind enveloped in dark cloud,
come to us.

With the dark thunder above you, high-
flying, come to us.

With the shaped cloud at your feet, high-
flying, come to us.

With the distant darkness made of dark cloud
over your head, come to us.

With the distant darkness made of male rain
over your head, come to us.

With the distant darkness made of female rain
over your head, come to us.

With the zigzag lightning flung out high over
your head, come to us.

With the rainbow hanging high over your
head, come to us.

With the distant darkness made of dark cloud
on the tips of your wings, come to us.

With the distant darkness made of the male
rain at the tips of your wings, flying high,
come to us.

With the distant darkness made of the dark
mist at the tips of your wings, flying high,
come to us.

With the distant darkness made of the female
rain at the tips of your wings, flying high,
come to us.

With the zigzag lightning flung out high on
the tips of your wings, come to us.

With the rainbow hanging high on the tips of
your wings, come to us.

With the near darkness made of the dark
cloud, of the male rain, of the dark mist, of
the female rain, come to us.

With the darkness of the earth, come to us.

With these I wish for the foam floating on the
water flowing over the roots of the great
corn.

I have made sacrifice for you.

I have prepared smoke for you.

Restore my feet for me.

Restore my limbs for me.

Restore my body for me.

Restore my mind for me.

Restore my voice for me.

Take your spell out for me today.

Take your spell away for me today.

You have taken it away from me.

It is taken far away from me.

You have taken it far off.

In beauty I recover.

In beauty my inside becomes cool.

In beauty my eyes regain their sight.

In beauty I regain the use of my limbs.

In beauty I hear again.

In beauty the spell is lifted.

In beauty I walk.

Impervious to pain, I walk.

My insides light, I walk.

I walk with lively feelings.

In beauty, I desire abundant dark clouds.

In beauty, I desire dark mists.

In beauty, I desire passing showers.

In beauty, I desire plants of all kinds.

In beauty, I desire pollen.

In beauty, I desire dew.

In beauty, may lovely white corn accompany
you to the ends of the earth.

In beauty, may lovely yellow corn accompany
you to the ends of the earth.

In beauty, may lovely blue corn accompany
you to the ends of the earth.

In beauty, may corn of all kinds accompany
you to the ends of the earth.

In beauty, may beautiful plants of all kinds
accompany you to the ends of the earth.

In beauty, may beautiful goods accompany
you to the ends of the earth.

In beauty, may beautiful jewels accompany
you to the ends of the earth.

With these in front of you, may they come
with you in beauty.

With these in front of you, in beauty may
they come with you.

With these behind you, may they come with
you in beauty.

With these below you, may they come with
you in beauty.

With these above you, may they come with
you in beauty.

With these all around you, may they come
with you in beauty.

In this way you accomplish your tasks in beauty.

Old men will look at you happily.

Young men will look at you happily.

The young women will look at you happily.

The boys will look at you happily.

The girls will look at you happily.

The children will look at you happily.

The chief men will look at you happily.

Happily, dispersing in different directions,
they will look at you.

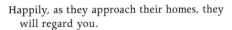

Happily, as they approach their homes, they
    will regard you.

Happily, may their roads home be on the trail
    of pollen.

Again I walk in beauty,

with beauty before me,

with beauty behind me,

with beauty below me.

With beauty above me,

with beauty all around me, I walk.

It is finished again in beauty.

It is finished again in beauty.

It is finished again in beauty.

It is finished again in beauty.

Prayer of the first dancers,
from The Ceremony of the Night Chant

The Earth is our Mother

A long time ago the earth was placed here for us, the people, the Navajo; it gives us corn and we consider her our mother.

... The Earth is our mother. The white man is ruining our mother. I don't know the white man's ways but to us the Mesa, the air, the water, are Holy Elements. We pray to these Holy Elements in order for our people to flourish and perpetuate the well-being of each generation.

Even when we are small, our cradle is made from the things given to us from Mother Earth. We use these elements all of our lives and when we die we go back to Mother Earth.

When we were first put on earth, the herbs and medicine were also put here for us to use. These have become part of our prayers to Mother Earth. We should realize it for if we forget these things we will vanish as the people. That is why I don't like the coal mine.

Asa Bazhonoodah

[From a speech given in Washington in spring 1971 during Senate hearings on open-pit mining on Black Mesa.]

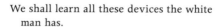

We shall learn all these devices the white
   man has.

We shall handle his tools for ourselves.

We shall master his machinery and his
   inventions, his skills, his medicine, his
   planning.

But we'll retain our beauty

And still be Indian.

NEZ PERCÉ

All Men Are Brothers

Whenever the white man treats the Indian as they
treat each other, then we will have no more wars. We
shall all be alike – brothers of one father and one
mother, with one sky above us and one country
around us, and one government for all.

Chief Joseph (Hinmaton Yalatkit), 1830–1904

My friends, I have been asked to show my heart. I am
glad to have a chance to do so. I want the white

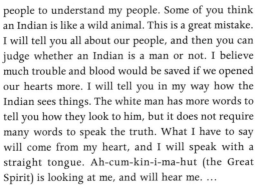

people to understand my people. Some of you think an Indian is like a wild animal. This is a great mistake. I will tell you all about our people, and then you can judge whether an Indian is a man or not. I believe much trouble and blood would be saved if we opened our hearts more. I will tell you in my way how the Indian sees things. The white man has more words to tell you how they look to him, but it does not require many words to speak the truth. What I have to say will come from my heart, and I will speak with a straight tongue. Ah-cum-kin-i-ma-hut (the Great Spirit) is looking at me, and will hear me. ...

Our fathers gave us many laws, which they had learned from their fathers. These laws were good. They told us to treat all men as they treated us; that we should never be the first to break a bargain; that it was a disgrace to tell a lie; that we should speak only the truth; that it was a shame for one man to take from another his wife, or his property without paying for it. We were taught to believe that the Great Spirit sees and hears everything, and that he never forgets; that hereafter he will give every man a spirit-home according to his desserts: if he has been a good man, he will have a good home; if he has been a bad man, he will have a bad home. This I believe, and all my people believe the same. ...

All men were made by the same Great Spirit Chief. They are all brothers. The earth is the mother of all people, and all people should have equal rights upon it. You might as well expect the rivers to run backward as that any man who was born a free man should be contented penned up and denied liberty to go where he pleases. If you tie a horse to a stake, do you expect he will grow fat? If you pen an Indian up on a small spot of earth, and compel him to stay there, he will not be contented nor will he grow and prosper. I have asked some of the great white chiefs where they get their authority to say to the Indian that he shall stay in one place, while he sees white men going where they please. They cannot tell me.

From a speech by Chief Joseph, 1879

OJIBWA

On Tradition

Among the Indians there have been no written laws. Customs handed down from generation to generation have been the only laws to guide them. Every one might act different from what was considered right

did he choose to do so, but such acts would bring
upon him the censure of the Nation … This fear of
the Nation's censure acted as a mighty band, binding
all in one social, honourable compact.

George Copway (Chief Kah-ge-ga-gah-bowh), 1818–63

Love of Nature

I was born in *Nature's wide domain!* The trees were
all that sheltered my infant limbs – the blue heavens
all that covered me. I am one of Nature's children; I
have always admired her; she shall be my glory; her
features – her robes, and the wreath about her brow
– the seasons – her stately oaks, and the evergreen –
her hair, ringlets over the earth – all contribute to my
enduring love of her; and wherever I see her,
emotions of pleasure roll in my breast, and swell and
burst like waves on the shores of the ocean, in prayer
and praise to Him who has placed me in her hand. It
is thought great to be born in palaces, surrounded
with wealth – but to be born in Nature's wide domain
is greater still!

George Copway

Innovocations of the Sun and the Moon

1

The father of the day can never fail us, he who makes everything vegetate, and without whom cold, darkness and horror would everywhere prevail.

Beautiful, all-seeing, all penetrating luminary! Without whose influence the mind of man has neither efficacy nor vigour.

Sun! Be thou favourable to us in this point, as thou are in that of our hunting, when we beseech thee to guide us in quest of our daily support.

2

Beautiful spouse of the sun! Give us to discover the tracks of elks, moose-deer, martins, lynxes and bears, when urged by our wants, we pursue by night the hunt after these beasts. Give to our women the strength to support the pains of childbirth, render their wombs prolific, and their breasts inexhaustible fountains.

Anon

OMAHA

Myth

Toward the coming of the sun

There the people of every kind gathered,

And great animals of every kind.

Truly all gathered together, all,

Even insects of every description,

Truly all gathered there together,

By what means or manner we know not.

Truly, one alone of all these was the greatest,

Inspiring to all minds,

The great white rock,

Standing and reaching as high as the heavens,
    wrapped in mist,

Truly as high as the heavens.

Thus my little ones shall speak of me,

As long as they shall travel in life's path,

Thus may they speak of me.

Such were the words, it has been said.

Then next in rank

Thou, male of the crane, stood with thy long
beak

And thy neck, none so long,

There with thy beak did thou strike the earth.

This shall be the legend

Of the people of the beginning, the red
people,

Thus my little ones shall speak of me.

Then next in rank stood the male gray wolf,
whose cry,

Though uttered without effort, truly made the
earth tremble,

Even the solid earth to tremble.

Invoking the Powers

Remember, remember the circle of the sky

    the stars and the brown eagle

    the super natural winds

    breathing night and day

    from the four directions

Remember, remember the great life of the sun

    breathing on the earth

    it lies upon the earth

    to bring out life upon the earth

    life covering the earth

Remember, remember the sacredness of things

    running streams and dwellings

    the young within the nest

    a hearth with sacred fire

    the holy flame of fire

ONONDAGA

Power is not manifested in the human being. True power is in the Creator. If we continue to ignore the message by which we exist and we continue to destroy the source of our lives then our children will suffer ... I must warn you that the Creator made us all equal with one another. And not only human beings, but all life is equal. The equality of our life is what you must understand and the principles by which you must continue on behalf of the future of this world. Economics and technology may assist you, but they will also destroy you if you do not use the principles of equality. Profit and loss will mean nothing to your future generations ...

I do not see a delegation for the four-footed. I see no seat for the eagles. We forget and we consider ourselves superior, but we are after all a mere part of the Creation. And we must continue to understand where we are. And we stand between the mountain and the ant, somewhere and there only, as part and parcel of the Creation. It is our responsibility, since we have been given the minds to take care of these things. The elements and the animals, and the birds, they live in a state of grace. They are absolute, they can do no wrong. Is it only we, the two-leggeds, that can do this. And when we do this to our brothers, to

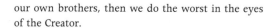

our own brothers, then we do the worst in the eyes
of the Creator.

Oren Lyons
From an address delivered to the United Nations, 1977

A Sacred Trust

Being born as humans to this earth is a very sacred
trust. We have a sacred responsibility because of the
special gift we have, which is beyond the fine gifts
of the plant life, the fish, the woodlands, the birds,
and all the other living things on earth. We are able
to take care of them.

Audrey Shenandoah, 1987

A Blessing

Bless the man who preserves his Selfhood ever calm
and unshaken by the storms of existence – not a leaf,
as it were, astir on the tree; not a ripple upon the
surface of the shining pool – his mind.

Anon

Your Path

Everything is laid out for you.

Your path is straight ahead of you.

Sometimes it's invisible but it's there.

You may not know where it's going,

but you have to follow that path.

It's the path to the Creator.

It's the only path there is.

Chief Leon Shenandoah, 1990

OSAGE

The Puma Speaks

It has been said that,

at that time and place, in this house,

the Honga, a people who possess seven fireplaces,

spoke to the one who had made his body of the
Puma,

saying: O grandfather,

we have nothing that is fit for use as a symbol.

The Puma replied quickly: Little ones,

you say you have nothing for use as a symbol,

but I am one who is fitted for use as a symbol.

Look at the male puma, lying on the earth.

I am the one who has made his body of the male
puma.

The knowledge of my courage has spread over the
land.

Look at the god of day, who sits in the heavens.

I am a person who sits close to the god of day.

When the little ones make their bodies of me

they shall always be free from all causes of death

as they travel life's path.

Look at the great red boulder that sits on the
earth.

I am the person who draws to himself the power of
that boulder.

Even the gods themselves stumble

over me as I sit immovable.

When the little ones make their bodies of me

even the gods will trip over them, and fall.

Even the great gods themselves

as they move over the earth pass around me

as I sit immovable as the great red boulder.

When the little ones make their bodies of me

even the gods themselves shall pass around them

in forked lines as they travel life's path.

Even the great gods themselves

are afraid to stare at me insolently.

When the little ones make their bodies of me

even the gods will be afraid

to stare them in the face as they travel life's path.

It has been said, at that time and place,

in this house, he said to them: Behold,

the Black Bear, without blemish, that lies on the
earth.

I am a person who has made his body of the Black
Bear.

See the god of night who sits in the heavens.

I am the person who makes the Black Bear draw
  his power from the god of night.

Regard the great black boulder that sits on the
  earth.

I am a person who sits next to the great black
  boulder.

Regard the great black boulder that sits on the
  earth.

When the little ones make their bodies of the great
  black boulder

even the great gods themselves

shall stumble over them and fall.

Even the gods themselves

as they move over the earth pass around me in
  forked lines as I sit immovable as the great black
  boulder.

When the little ones make their bodies of me

even the gods themselves

shall pass around them in forked lines as they
  travel the path of life.

Truly, at that time and place, in this house, it has
  been said

that he said to them: Regard the great white swan.

I am a person who has made his body of the great
  white swan.

Look at the god of night, the Male Star, the
  Morning Star.

I am a person who has made his body of the god of
  night.

Regard the great white boulder that sits on the earth.

I am a person who has made his body of the great
  white boulder.

When the little ones make their bodies of me

even the great gods themselves

shall stumble over them and fall.

Even the gods themselves

as they move over the earth pass around me as I sit
  immovable as the great white boulder.

When the little ones make their bodies of me

even the gods themselves

shall pass around them as they pass around the
  great white boulder.

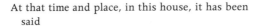

At that time and place, in this house, it has been
said

that he said to them: Behold the bull elk who sits
on the earth.

I am the person who makes the bull elk draw his
power from the yellow boulder.

Behold the Female Star, the evening star.

I am the person who makes the yellow boulder
draw its power from the evening star.

When the little ones make their bodies of me

even the great gods themselves

shall stumble over them and fall.

Even the gods themselves

as they move over the earth pass around me as I sit
immovable as the great yellow boulder.

When the little ones make their bodies of me

even the gods themselves

shall pass around them as they pass around the
great yellow boulder.

Even the gods themselves

are afraid to bite me in anger.

When the little ones make their bodies of me

the gods themselves will be afraid to bite them in
anger.

From 'The Sending', in Francis La Flesche,
The Osage Tribe: The Rite of Vigil

The Planting Song

I have made a footprint, a sacred one.

I have made a footprint; through it the blades
push upward.

I have made a footprint; through it the blades
radiate.

I have made a footprint; over it the blades float in
the wind.

I have made a footprint; over it the ears lean
toward one another.

I have made a footprint; over it I pluck the ears.

I have made a footprint; over it I bend the stalk to
pluck the ears.

I have made a footprint; over it the blossoms lie
gray.

I have made a footprint; smoke arises from my house.

I have made a footprint; there is a cheer in
my house.

I have made a footprint; I live in the light of day.

Wi'gi-e of the Symbolic Painting

With what shall they adorn their bodies, as they
tread the path of life? it has been said, in this
house.

The crimson color of the God of Day who sitteth in
the heavens,

They shall make to be their sacred color, as they
go forth upon life's journey.

Verily, the God who reddens the heavens as he
approaches,

They shall make to be their sacred color, as they
go forth upon life's journey.

When they adorn their bodies with the crimson
hue shed by that God of Day,

Then shall the little ones make themselves to be free

From all causes of death, as they go forth on life's journey.

What shall the people use for a symbolic plume?

They said to one another, it has been said, in this house.

Verily, the God who always comes out at the beginning of day,

Has at his right side

A beam of light that stands upright like a plume.

That beam of light shall the people make to be their sacred plume.

What shall they place as a pendant upon his breast?

They said to one another.

The shell of the mussel who sitteth upon the earth,

They shall place as a pendant upon his breast.

It is as the God of Day who sitteth in the heavens,

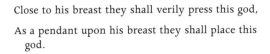

Close to his breast they shall verily press this god,

As a pendant upon his breast they shall place this
god.

Then shall the little ones become free from all
causes

Of death, as they go forth upon life's journey.

From Francis La Flesche,
The Osage Tribe: The Rite of Vigil

[This rite was performed in times of distress in order to
bring the people in close touch with the Supernatural
Power. It can be observed individually as well as collec-
tively. At any time during the summer – when nature is
'fully awake and active' – the man stricken with grief by
the loss of a beloved person may take upon himself this
rite in seeking pity from the Mysterious Power. The Osage
Indian, whose life is replete with sun-symbolism, experi-
ences the sun as the visible manifestation of the Highest
Power; above all, he glorifies the regularity of the
movements of the 'God of Day.']

PAIUTE

Tradition

The traditions of our people are handed down from father to sun. The chief is considered to be the most learned, and the leader of the tribe. The doctor, however, is thought to have more inspiration. He is supposed to be in communion with spirits ... He cures the sick by the laying on of hands, and prayers and incantations and heavenly songs. He infuses new life into the patient, and performs most wonderful feats of skill in his practice ... He clothes himself in the skins of young, innocent animals, such as the fawn; and decorates himself with the plumage of harmless birds, such as the dove and the humming-bird ...

Sarah Winnemucca, 1844–91

PAPAGO

Names and Naming

A shaman has a dream and names a child for what he dreams in it. Among such names are Circling Light, Rushing Light Beams, Daylight Comes, Wind Rainbow, Wind Leaves, Rainbow Shaman, Feather Leaves, A-Rainbow-as-a-Bow, Shining Beetle, Singing Dawn, Hawk-flying-over-Water-Holes, Flowers Trembling, Chief-of-Jackrabbits, Water-Drops-on-Leaves, Short Wings, Leaf Blossom, Foamy Water.

Thanksgiving Prayer

Evil of the people

but the Great Ones being good

were good to us

though they came among us

to punish us

in their goodness and kindness

they granted us forgiveness

Now this night

made sacred by the Great Ones

being among us

can remind us

to give each other kindness

and helpfulness

to be going on in harmony and peace

as Children of the Great Ones

Walk Proud, Walk Straight, Let Your Thoughts Race

Walk proud, walk straight, let your thoughts race with the blue wind, but do not bare your soul to your enemies.

Patty Harjo

Song of Encouragement

Within my bowl there lies

Shining dizziness,

Bubbling drunkenness.

There are great whirlwinds
Standing upside down above us.
They lie within my bowl.

A great bear heart,
A great eagle heart,
A great hawk heart,
A great twisting wind –
All these have gathered here
And lie within my bowl.

Now you will drink it.

Beliefs

Hear now the words that make the stalk
  of the heart to blossom
    and our steps to reel.

For I made him from a stick of driftwood;

With the breath of the sun I gave him life.

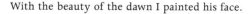

With the beauty of the dawn I painted his face.

And with the last shadows of the darkness I
marked lines upon it.

From the wing feathers of the great birds I made
his headdress,

and the butterflies lit, fanning their wings among
the feathers.

From the rainbow I made his bow, and from the
Milky Way his arrow.

I gave him gray fog as a mantle upon his shoulders,
and strong wind as a girdle about his waist.

From Navitcu (saguaro cactus) ceremony

PASSAMAQUODDY

Star Song

We are the singing stars,

We sing with our light.

We are the birds of fire,

Through the heavens we take our flight.

Our light is as a star,

Making a road for spirits.

Among us are three hunters

Forever chasing a bear.

There never was a time

When they three were not hunting.

We look down upon the mountains.

Trans. Charles Godfrey Leland
and John Dyneley Prince

PAWNEE

The Coming of the Corn

Give heed! Give heed!
Give heed, O ye People!
Unto the Abode of Life give ye heed,
And unto the Powers thereof
Let your hearts be turned in reverence ...

Life up your gaze!
Unto the blue and doming Skies
Lift up your gaze –
Where dwelleth the Father of Heaven,
Where dwelleth the Father of Life,
Yea, from everlasting to everlasting.
Lift up your gaze
Unto the Father! ...

In the Circle of the Heavens He hath set
The manifestations of His glory –

The bright and shining Sun,

Which giveth forth the Light of Day

And answereth the hymn wherewith His
creatures

Waken at Morn –

In the Circle of the Heavens He hath
established the Sun

To be a sign of His presence by Day,

And the quiet Stars hath He set to be His
nightly ministers ...

Anon

The Birth of Dawn

Earth our mother, breathe forth life

all night sleeping

now awaking

in the east

now see the dawn

Earth our mother, breathe and waken

    leaves are stirring

    all things moving

    new day coming

    life renewing

Eagle soaring, see the morning

    see the new mysterious morning

    something marvelous and sacred

    though it happens every day

    Dawn the child of God and Darkness

Adapted from Alice C. Fletcher, 'The Hako, a Pawnee
Ceremony', 22nd Annual BAE Report, 1904

Is This Real?

Let us see, is this real,

Let us see, is this real,

This life I am living?

You, Gods, who dwell everywhere,

Let us see, is this real,

This life I am living?

From Daniel G. Brinton, *Essays of an Americanist*

[This is, says Brinton, a war song with a curious metaphysical turn. It is sung when a warrior goes out all alone on the warpath from which it is likely he will never return.]

The Heavens Are Speaking

I stood there, I stood there,

The clouds are speaking.

I say, 'You are the ruling power,

I do not understand, I only know what I am told,

You are ruling power, you are now speaking,

This power is yours, O heavens.'

It is there that our hearts are set,

In the expanse of the heavens.

From Frances Densmore, *Pawnee Music*

[Before recording the first song Frances Densmore's informant spoke the following sentences, accompanying the words with slow drum beats: 'The song which I am about to sing belonged to Man Chief. When he became chief he used to go out into the storm … He heard Tirawa speak through the clouds. He knew the heavens were the ruling power, and he prayed for his people.']

Good and Evil

All things in the world are two, In our minds we are two – good and evil. With our eyes we see two things – things that are fair and things that are ugly … We have the right hand that strikes and makes for evil, and the left hand full of kindness, near the heart. One foot may lead us to an evil way, the other foot may lead us to a good. So are all things two, all two.

Eagle Chief (Letakots-Lesa), late 19th century

The Hako Party Presented to the Powers

Look down, West gods, look upon us! We gaze afar on your dwelling.

Look down while here we are standing, look down upon us, ye mighty!

Ye thunder gods, now behold us!

Ye lightning gods, now behold us!

Ye that bring life, now behold us!

Ye that bring death, now behold us!

Look down, South gods, look upon us!
  We gaze afar on your dwelling.

Look down while here we are standing,
  look down upon us, ye mighty!

Ye daylight gods, now behold us!

Ye sunshine gods, now behold us!

Ye increase gods, now behold us!

Ye plenty gods, now behold us!

Look down, North gods, look upon us!
  We gaze afar on your dwelling.

Look down while here we are standing,
  look down upon us, ye mighty!

Ye darkness gods, now behold us!

Ye moonlight gods, now behold us!

Ye that direct, now behold us!

Ye that discern, now behold us!

Daylight

Day is here! Day is here, is here!

Arise, my son, lift thine eyes. Day is here! Day
is here, is here!

Day is here! Day is here, is here!

Look up, my son and see the day. Day is here!
Day is here, is here!

Day is here! Day is here, is here!

Lo, the deer! Lo, the deer, the deer

Comes from her covert of the night! Day is
here! Day is here, is here!

Lo, the deer! Lo, the deer, the deer!

All creatures wake and see the light. Day is
here! Day is here, is here!

Day is here! Day is here, is here!

The Sixteen Circuits of the Lodge – Third Song

O'er the prairie flits in ever widening circles the shadow of a bird about me as I walk;
   Upward turn my eyes, Kawas looks upon me, she turns with flapping wings and far away she flies.

Round about a tree in ever widening circles an eagle flies, alertly watching o'er his nest;
   Loudly whistles he, a challenge sending afar, o'er the country wide it echoes, there defying foes.

The End of the World

Our people were made by the stars. When the time comes for all things to end, our people will turn into small stars and will fly to the South Star, where they belong. When the time comes for the ending of the world, the stars will again fall to the earth. They will mix among the people, for it will be a message to the people to get ready to be turned into stars.

Young Bull (Pitahauerat Pawnee)

[He was described in 1906 as 'the leading medicine-man among the Pitahauerat'.]

Resurrection

Now

you have come to listen,

Long Person,

you are staying right here,

Helper of Humans,

you never relax your grip,

you never let go your grip on the soul.

You have taken a firm hold on the soul.

I originated at the cataract, not so far away.

I will stretch out my hand to where you are.

My soul has come to bathe in your body.

The white foam will cling to my head

as I go on with my life,

the white staff will come into my outstretched
   hand.

The fire in the hearth will be left burning for me.

The soul has been raised gradually to the
   seventh upper world.

Anon

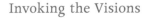

Invoking the Visions

Holy visions!

Hither come, we pray you, come unto us,

Bringing with you joy;

Come, O come to us, holy visions,

Bringing with you joy.

Holy visions!

Near are they approaching, near to us here,

Bringing with them joy;

Nearer still they come – holy visions –

Bringing with them joy.

Holy visions!

Lo! Before the doorway pause they, waiting,

Bearing gifts of joy;

Pausing there they wait – holy visions –

Bearing gifts of joy.

Holy visions!
Now they cross the threshold, gliding softly
Toward the space within;
Softly gliding on – holy visions –
Toward the space within.

Holy visions!
They the lodge are filling with their presence,
Fraught with hope and peace;
Filling all the lodge – holy visions –
Fraught with hope and peace.

Holy visions!
Now they touch the children, gently touch
   them
Giving dreams of joy;
Gently touch each one – holy visions –
Giving dreams of joy.

Holy visions!

Ended now their mission, pass they outward,
Yet they leave us joy;
Pass they all from us – holy visions –
Yet they leave us joy.

Holy visions!
They, the sky ascending, reach their dwelling;
There they rest above;
They their dwelling reach – holy visions –
There they rest above.

PEQUOT

How they go to work to enslave a free people, and call
it religion, is beyond the power of my imagination …

William Apess, 1836

Song of an Initiate

climbed the blue staircase up to sky
climbed where the roses were opening
   where roses were speaking

heard nothing   nothing to hear
   heard silence

i climbed the roses were singing
   where the gods were waiting
   blue staircase up in the sky

but heard nothing   nothing to hear
   heard silence   silence

Anon

PIMA

The Creation of the Earth

Earth Magician shapes this world.

 Behold what he can do!

Round and smooth he moulds it.

 Behold what he can do!

Earth Magician makes the mountains.

 Heed what he has to say!

He it is that makes the mesas.

 Heed what he has to say.

Earth Magician shapes this world;

 Earth Magician makes its mountains;

Of all the birds of summer,

With these four times I gave my plume wands
 human form.

With the flesh of the one who is my mother,

Cotton wool,

Even a poorly made cotton thread,

Four times encircling them and tying it about
   their bodies,

I gave the plume wands human form.

With the flesh of the one who is our mother,

Black paint woman,

Four times covering them with flesh,

I gave my plume wands human form.

In a short time the plume wands were ready.

Taking the plume wands,

I made my road go forth.

Yonder with prayers

We took our road.

Thinking, 'Let it be here,'

Our earth mother

We passed upon her road.

Our fathers,

There on your earth mother,

There where you are waiting your plume
   wands

We have passed you on your roads.

There where you are all gathered together in
  beauty

Now that you are to receive your plume
  wands,

You are gathered together.

This day I give you plume wands.

By means of your supernatural wisdom

You will clothe yourself with the plume
  wands.

Wherever you abide permanently,

Your little wind-blown cloud,

Your thin wisps of cloud,

Your hanging stripes of cloud,

Your massed up clouds, replete with living
  waters,

You will send forth to stay with us.

They will come out standing on all sides.

With your fine rain caressing the earth,

With your weapons, the lightning,

With your rumbling thunder,

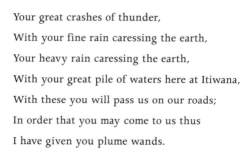

Your great crashes of thunder,

With your fine rain caressing the earth,

Your heavy rain caressing the earth,

With your great pile of waters here at Itiwana,

With these you will pass us on our roads;

In order that you may come to us thus

I have given you plume wands.

My fathers,

When you have taken your plume wands,

With your waters,

Your seeds,

Your riches,

Your power,

Your strong spirit,

With all your good fortune whereof you are
possessed,

Me you will bless.

POTAWOMI

The Act of Creation

As he stood upon the shores thereof in the presence of them all, His eyes flashed waw-saw mowin (lightning)! The late became boiling water! The earth trembled! He then spake in the voice of thunder; 'Come forth, ye Lords of Au-kee (the world)!' The ground opened. And from out of the red clay that lined the lake came forth au-ne-ne gaie ik-we (man and woman) … The bride and groom then each other fondly kissed as hand in hand they stood, in naked innocence, in the full bloom of youth … They looked all about them in wonder and surprise.

Chief Pokagon, d. 1841

Reflections

Now let us all as one pray the Great Spirit that he will open the eyes of their understanding and teach them to know that we are human as well as they; teach them to know that

Within the recess of the native's soul

There is a secret place, which god doth hold;

And though the storms of life do war around,

Yet still within His image fixed is found.

I am getting to be an old man. I often feel one foot is uplifted to step into the world beyond. But I am thankful that the measure of my days has been lengthened out, that I am able to stand before you in this great congress of people, in this four hundredth year of the white man's advent in our fathers' land.

…

When I am gone I wish no stone to rise above my last resting-place as oft is done, to tell, not what men were, but what they should have been. However, I desire to leave upon the printed page an epitaph which all may read. That shall be my most solemn protest and prayer against the introduction of alcohol in any form among my people; and to accomplish that desire of my heart I see no hope except by the complete overthrow of the rum-shop and the destruction of all that can intoxicate, together with cigarettes, the father and mother of palsy and cancer.

Chief Pokagon

The Veil of Time

Often in the stillness of the night, when all nature seems asleep about me, there comes a gentle rapping at the door of my heart. I open it; and a voice enquires 'Pokagon, what of your people? What will their future be?' My answer is; 'Mortal man has not the power to draw aside the veil of unborn time to tell the future of his race. That gift belongs of the Divine alone. But it is given to him to closely judge the future by the present and the past.'

Simon Pokagon, 1830–99

SENECA

My Great Father: I have traveled a great distance to see you – I have seen you and my heart rejoices. I have heard your words – they have entered one ear and shall not escape the other, and I will carry them to my people as pure as they came from your mouth.

My Great Father: I am going to speak the truth. The Great Spirit looks down upon us, and I can call Him to witness all that may pass between us on this occasion. If I am here now and have seen your people, your houses, your vessels on the big lake, and a great many wonderful things far beyond my comprehension, which appear to have been made by the Great Spirit and placed in your hands. I am indebted to my Father here, who invited me from home, under whose wings I have been protected. Yes, my Great Father, I have traveled with your chief; I have followed him, and trod in his tracks; but there is still another Great Father to whom I am much indebted – it is the Father of us all. Him who made us and placed us on this earth. I feel grateful to the Great Spirit for strengthening my heart for such an undertaking, and for preserving the life which he gave me. The Great Spirit made us all – he made my skin red, and yours white; he placed us on this earth, and intended that we should live differently from each other.

Chief Red Jacket, from 'It Is Too Soon, My Great Father, to Send Those Good Men Among Us'

Brother! You say there is but one way to worship and serve the Great Spirit. If there is but one religion, why do you white people differ so much about it? Why not all agree, as you can all read the book?

Brother we do not understand these things. We are told that your religion was given to your forefathers and has been handed down, father to son. We also

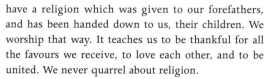

have a religion which was given to our forefathers, and has been handed down to us, their children. We worship that way. It teaches us to be thankful for all the favours we receive, to love each other, and to be united. We never quarrel about religion.

Brother! The Great Spirit has made us all. But he had made a great difference between his white and red children. He has given us a different complexion and different customs. To you he has given the arts; to these he has not opened our eyes. We know these things to be true. Since he has made so great a difference between us in other things, why may not we conclude that he has given us a different religion, according to our understanding? The Great Spirit does right. He knows what is best for his children. We are satisfied.

Brother! We do not wish to destroy your religion, or to take it from you. We only want to enjoy our own.

Brother! You say you have not come to get our land or our money, but to enlighten out minds. I will now tell you that I have been at your meetings and saw you collecting money from the meeting. I cannot tell what this money was intended for, but suppose it was for your minister; and if we should conform to your way of thinking, perhaps you may want some from us.

Chief Red Jacket
From a speech given in 1828

Thanksgiving

Sovereignty is something that goes in ever-widening circles, beginning with yourself ... If a person can go out into the stream and fish for their needs, if they can do whatever they have to do to provide for those who are dependent on them, then that is sufficient.

We return thanks to the moon and stars, which give us light when the sun has gone to rest. We thank thee, that thy wisdom has so kindly provided, that light is never wanting to us. Continue unto us this goodness.

We return thanks to the sun, that he has looked upon the earth with beneficent eye. We thank thee that thou hast, in thy unbounded wisdom, commanded the sun to regulate the return of the seasons, to dispense heat and cold, and to watch over the comfort of thy people. Give unto us that wisdom, which will guide us in the path of truth. Keep us from all evil ways, that the sun may never hide his face from us for shame and leave us in darkness.

Sose-ha-wa
From a traditional Thanksgiving address,
trans. Ha-sa-no-an-da/Ely Parker, 1851

SHAWNEE

Brothers – We all belong to one family; we are all children of the Great Spirit; we walk in the same path; slake our thirst at the same spring; and now affairs of the greatest concern lead us to smoke the pipe around the same council fire!

Brothers – We are friends; we must assist each other to bear our burdens. The blood of many of our fathers and brothers has run like water on the ground, to satisfy the avarice of the white men. We, ourselves, are threatened with a great evil; nothing will pacify them but the destruction of all the red men.

Brothers – When the white men first set foot on our grounds, they were hungry; they had no place on which to spread their blankets, or to kindle their fires. They were feeble; they could do nothing for themselves. Our fathers commiserated their distress, and shared freely with them whatever the Great Spirit had given his red children. They gave them food when hungry, medicine when sick, spread skins for them to sleep on, and gave them grounds, that they might hunt and raise corn.

Brothers – The white people are like poisonous serpents; when chilled, they are feeble, and harmless, but invigorate them with warmth, and they sting their benefactors to death ...

Brothers – The white men are not friends to the Indians; at first, they only asked for land sufficient for a wigwam; now, nothing will satisfy them but the whole of our hunting grounds, from the rising to the setting sun ...

Brothers – My people are brave and numerous; but the white people are too strong for them alone. I wish you to take up the tomahawk with them. If we all unite, we will cause the rivers to stain the great waters with their blood.

Brothers – If you do not unite with us, they will first destroy us, and then you will fall an easy prey to them. They have destroyed many nations of red men because they were not united, because they were not friends to each other.

Brothers – We must be united; we must smoke the same pipe; we must fight each other's battles; and more than all, we must love the Great Spirit; he is for us; he will destroy our enemies, and make his red children happy.

Chief Tecumseh, 1768–1813

SIOUX

Ghost Dance Song

They say

the spirit army is approaching,

the spirit army is approaching,

the whole world is moving onward,

the whole world is moving onward.

See, everybody is standing, watching.

Everybody is standing, watching.

The whole world is coming,

a nation is coming, a nation is coming.

The Eagle has brought the message to the people.

The father says so, the father says so.

Over the whole earth they are coming.

The buffalo are coming, the buffalo are coming.

The Crow has brought the message to the people,

the father says so, the father says so.

My children, my children,

it is I who wear the morning star on my head.

It is I who wear the morning star on my
  head.

I show it to my children.

I show it to my children.

Directions

Go to a mountaintop and cry for a vision.

Song of the Spirit Dance

Thus the Father saith,

Lo, he now commandeth

All on earth to sing,

To sing now.

Thus he hath spoken,

Thus he hath spoken.

Tell afar his message,

Tell afar his message!

The Horse

When I was somewhat past ten years of age, my father took me with him to watch the horses out on the prairie. We watered the herd and about the middle of the day came home for dinner ... While we sat watching the herd my father said: 'These horses are godlike, or mystery beings.'

Wolf Chief, Hidatsa Sioux, late 19th-century

DAKOTA
(Santee Sioux)

The Vital Concern

Science tells us that the native Americans came from northern Asia and that they may have arrived here from ten to twelve thousand years ago. But they were not the first inhabitants of this continent. From archaeological evidences we know that man-made implements of stone were left beside ancient campfires fifteen to eighteen thousand years ago, some even say twenty thousand. Man-made projectiles, too, have been found deep in the earth, together with the skeletons of a prehistoric species of bison.

It is known from such remains that these earlier peoples lived by both hunting and seed-gathering. We cannot know what became of them – whether they had all vanished before the ancestors of the modern Indians arrived, or whether some were still wandering about and were absorbed by the new-comers. Of course, every bit of this is speculative; one guess is nearly as good as another, for we can never be sure of what actually took place.

And it doesn't really matter, does it? All that which lies hidden in the remote past is interesting, to be sure, but not so important as the present and the future. The vital concern is not where a people came from, physically, but where they are going, spiritually.

From Ella Deloria, *Speaking of Indians*, 1944

War Song

Friend, whatever hardships threaten,

If thou call me,

I'll befriend thee;

All enduring fearlessly,

I'll befriend thee.

Humility

One major difference between our people and those of the
dominant society today is humility. Among our people,
no matter how far or how high a person goes, they know
they are small in the presence of God and universe.

Lincoln Tritt, 1989

Nature

We do not like to harm the trees. Whenever we can, we
always make an offering of tobacco to the trees before we
cut them down. We never waste the wood, but use all
that we cut down. If we did not think of their feelings,
and did not offer them we would be offending Nature.

Anon

The Great Spirit

… the voice of the Great Spirit is heard in the
twittering of birds, the rippling of mighty waters, and
the sweet breathing of flowers. If this is Paganism, then
at present, at least, I am a Pagan.

Gertrude Simmons Bonnin (Zitkala-Sa), 1876–1938

A Prayer

O ye people, be ye healed;

Life anew I bring unto ye.

O ye people, be ye healed;

Life anew I bring unto ye.

Through the Father over all

Do I thus.

Life anew I bring unto ye.

Good Eagle (Wanbli-Waste),
late 19th-century holy man

Creation

We believe that the spirit pervades all creation and
that every creature possesses a soul in some degree,
though not necessarily a soul conscious of itself. The
tree, the waterfall, the grizzly bear, each is an
embodied Force, and as such an object of reverence.

Charles A. Eastman (Ohiyesa), 1902

An Indian Boy

It seems to be a popular idea that all the characteristic skill of the Indian is instinctive and hereditary. This is a mistake. All the stoicism and patience of the Indian are acquired traits.

… My uncle would say to me, 'you ought to follow the example of the *shunktokesha* (wolf). Even when he is surprised and runs for his life, he will pause to take one more look at you before he enters his final retreat. So you must take a second look at everything you see.

'It is better to view animals unobserved. I have learned many of their secrets in this way. I was once the unseen spectator of a thrilling battle between a pair of grizzly bears and three buffaloes – a rash act for the bears, for it was in the moon of strawberries, when the buffaloes sharpen and polish their horns for bloody contests among themselves.

'I advise you, my boy, never to approach a grizzly's den from the front, but to steal up behind and throw your blanket or a stone in front of the hole. He does not usually rush for it, but first puts his head out and listens, and then comes out very indifferently and sits on his haunches on the mound in front of the hole before he makes any attack. While he is exposing himself in this fashion, aim at his heart. Always be as cool as the animal himself.' Thus he armed me against the cunning of savage beasts by teaching me how to outwit them.

'In hunting,' he would resume, 'you will be guided by the habits of the animal you seek. Remember that a moose stays in swampy or low land or between high mountains near a spring or lake, for thirty to sixty days at a time. Most large game moves about continually, except the doe in the spring; it is then a very easy matter to find her with the fawn. Conceal yourself in a convenient place as soon as you observe any signs of the presence of either and then call with your birchen doe-caller.

'Whichever one hears you first will soon appear in your neighbourhood. But you must be very watchful, or you may be made a fawn of by a large wild-cat. They understand the characteristic call of the doe perfectly well.

'When you have any difficulty with a bear or a wild-cat – that is, if the creature shows signs of attacking you – you must make him fully understand that you have seen him and are aware of his intentions. If you are not well equipped for a pitched battle, the only way to make him retreat is to take a long, sharp-pointed pole for a spear and rush towards him. No wild beast will face this unless he is cornered and already wounded. These fierce beasts are generally afraid of the common weapon of the larger animals – the horns, and if these are very strong and sharp, they dare not risk an open fight.

'There is one exception to this rule – the grey wolf will attack when very hungry. But their courage depends upon their numbers; in this they are like white men. One wolf or two will never attack a man. They will stampede a herd of buffaloes in order to get at the calves; they will rush upon a herd of antelopes, for these are helpless; but they are always careful about attacking man.'

Of this nature were the instructions of my uncle, who was widely known at that time as among the greatest hunters of his tribe.

All boys were expected to endure hardship without complaint. In savage warfare a young man must, of course, be an athlete and used to undergoing all sorts of privations. He must be able to go without food and water for two or three days without displaying any weakness, or to run for a day and a night without any rest. He must be able to traverse a pathless and wild country without losing his way either in the day or night time. He cannot refuse to do any of these things if he aspires to be a warrior.

Charles A. Eastman (Ohiyesa)
From *Indian Boyhood*, 1914

[Here at last we have the Indian speaking for himself for though Dr Charles Eastman, MD, had been practising medicine for many years under his American name, he was born a Sioux Indian when his people were still living the wild nomadic life which he has described so well in his books. He has done much for the Indians by his writings and lectures and by watching over their interests at Washington.]

On Work

When a man does a piece of work which is admired by all we say that it is wonderful; but when we see the changes of day and night, the sun, the moon and the stars in the sky, and the changing seasons upon the earth, with their ripening fruits, anyone must realize that it is the work of someone more powerful than man.

Chased-by-Bears, 1843–1915 Santee-Yanktonai

After Death

It is the general belief of the Indians that after a man dies his spirit is somewhere on the earth or in the sky, we do not know exactly where, but we are

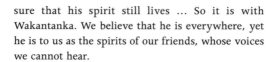

sure that his spirit still lives ... So it is with Wakantanka. We believe that he is everywhere, yet he is to us as the spirits of our friends, whose voices we cannot hear.

Chased-by-Bears

LAKOTA
(Teton Sioux)

In the cosmos of the tribes there was always the human element of chance, whereby a man or woman influences his or her life by acts of courage or wisdom. Man is finite, not infinite. To the tribal man, 'The name of the game is life.'

Anonymous Lakota educator

The Spring

Behold, my brothers, the spring has come, the earth has received the embraces of the sun and we shall soon see the results of that love!

Every seed is awakened and had all animal life. It is through this mysterious power that we too have our being and we therefore yield to our neighbors, even our animal neighbors, the same right as ourselves, to inhabit this land.

Sitting Bull (Tatanka Yotanka)
Hunkpapa Sioux

[Sitting Bull (David F. Barry), war chief and holy man, was born in 1831 and assassinated on 15 December 1890. He made this speech at a Powder River council in 1877.]

The Gift of a Child

It is strictly believed and understood by the Sioux that a child is the greatest gift from Wakan Tanka, in response to many devout prayers, sacrifices, and promises. Therefore the child is considered 'sent by Wakan Tanka', through some element – namely the element of human nature.

Robert Higheagle, early 20th century

A Medicine Man's Advice

When I was a young man I went to a medicine-man
for advice concerning my future. The medicine-man
said: 'I have not much to tell you except to help you
understand this earth on which you live. If a man is
to succeed on the hunt or the warpath, he must not
be governed by his inclination, but by an understanding of the ways of animals and of his natural
surroundings, gained through close observation. The
earth is large, and on it live many animals. The earth
is under the protection of something which at times
becomes visible to the eye.'

Lone Man (Isna la-wica), late 19th century

Self Reliance

… I have seen that in any great undertaking it is not
enough for a man to depend simply upon himself.

Lone Man (Isna la-wica)

On Birds

All birds, even those of the same species, are not alike, and it is the same with animals and with human beings. The reason Wakantanka does not make two birds, or animals, or human beings exactly alike is because each is placed here by Wakantanka to be an independent individuality and to rely upon itself.

Shooter, late 19th century

On Nature

I have noticed in my life that all men have a liking for some special animal, tree, plant or spot of earth. If men would pay more attention to those preferences and seek what is best to do in order to make themselves worthy of that toward which they are so attracted, they might have dreams which would purify their lives. Let a man decide upon his favorite animal and make a study of it, learning its innocent ways. Let him learn to understand its sounds and motions. The animals want to communicate with man but Wakantanka does not intend they shall do so directly – man must do the greater part in securing an understanding.

Brave Buffalo, late 19th-century medicine man

In a Sacred Manner I Live

In a sacred manner

I live

to the heavens

I gazed

in a sacred manner

I live

my horses

are many

Bear Eagle (Mato-wanbli)

[Bear Eagle learned this song from Shell Necklace (Panke-ska-napin). It is one of over 200 songs recorded at Standing Rock Reservation between 1911 and 1914 by Frances Densmore and her Sioux interpreter and assistant, Robert P. Higheagle.]

Prayer of the Foster-Parent Chant

Great Mystery, you have existed from
  the first;

This sky and this earth you created.

Wing flapper (Thunder Bird), you have
  existed from the first,

Your nation is half soldiers and half chiefs,
  so they say.

Lend me a good day; I borrow it.

Me, the Indian race, you have uplifted.

But now I am in despair;

Yet this good boy will renew the life of
  his people.

So, Great Mystery, look upon me; pity me,

That the nation may live –

Before the face of the North, the nation
  may live.

OGLALA

A Star Whisper

I had a vision. It came from the morning star, a star whisper. I heard this voice saying, 'Any understanding you ask from the morning star shall be granted to you, but ask with the sacred things, the drum, the sacred tobacco, the sacred sweet grass, and, above all, with the sacred pip.' Our dead sleep not. They tell me what I want to know. I have the power to see through things. I have only limited vision with the eyes I have in my head, but with my spiritual eyes I can see across oceans. The pipe is here to unite us, to remove the fences people put up against one another. Putting up fences is the white man's way. He invented the barbed wire, the barbed wire of the heart. The pipe is a fence remover. Sitting in a circle, smoking it the right way, all barriers disappear. Walls crumble.

Leonard Crow Dog (Kangi Shunka Manitou)

[Born in 1942, Leonard Crow Dog was spiritual leader of AIM, the American Indian Movement. He published his family autobiography in 1995, in collaboration with writer Richard Erdoes.]

Prophecies on a Circular Wing

They Will Return

They will return again.

All over the Earth,

They are returning again.

Ancient teachings of the Earth,

Ancient songs of the Earth.

They are returning again.

My friend, they are returning.

I give them to you,

And through them

You will understand,

You will see.

They are returning again

Upon the Earth.

Crazy Horse, 1842–77

Our Way of Life

Out of the Indian approach to life there came a great freedom – an intense and absorbing love for nature; a respect for life; enriching faith in a Supreme Power; and principles of truth, honesty, generosity, equity, and brotherhood as a guide to mundane relations.

Chief Luther Standing Bear, 1868–1939

So if today I had a young mind to direct, to start on the journey of life, and I was faced with the duty of choosing between the natural way of my forefathers and that of the white man's present way of civilisation, I would, for its welfare, unhesitatingly set that child's feet in the path of my forefathers. I would raise him to be an Indian!

Chief Luther Standing Bear

'Very early in life', says Standing Bear, 'the child began to realize that wisdom was all about and everywhere and that there were many things to know. There was no such thing as emptiness in the world. Even in the sky there were no vacant places. Everywhere there was life, visible and invisible, and every object possessed something that would be good for us to have also — even to the very stones. This gave a great interest to life. Even without human companionship one was never alone.' Such is his beginning. Then he goes on to show how it was that an Indian boy became acquainted with this world — not his world only, but his father's, his mother's, his people's world also, and every living creature's. It was a valuable world because so many beings shared it; it was a precious world, not to be walked in carelessly, and never to be looked on with contempt. All life, including human life, was valuable to an Indian, with the result that he managed his days with temperance, brought up his children neither with effort nor with neglect, killed animals reverently and delicately for their flesh or fur, kept the peace whenever possible, and frequently held communication with those spirits who for him represented the sentient, controlling Whole. He was always busy, never bored, and if Standing Bear is right in what he remembers, almost invariably happy.

It is this loss of faith that has left a void in Indian life — a void that civilization cannot fill. The old life was attuned to nature's rhythm — bound in mystical ties to the sun, moon and stars; to the waving grasses, flowing streams and whispering winds. It is not a question (as so many white writers like to state it) of

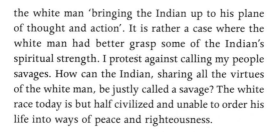

the white man 'bringing the Indian up to his plane of thought and action'. It is rather a case where the white man had better grasp some of the Indian's spiritual strength. I protest against calling my people savages. How can the Indian, sharing all the virtues of the white man, be justly called a savage? The white race today is but half civilized and unable to order his life into ways of peace and righteousness.

Chief Luther Standing Bear
From 'The Tragedy of the Sioux',
American Mercury 24, no. 95, 1931

The American Indian

The American Indian is of the soil, whether it be the region of the forests, plains, pueblos, or mesas. He fits into the landscape, for the hand that fashioned the continent also fashioned the man for his surroundings. He once grew as naturally as the wild sunflowers; he belongs just as the buffalo belonged ...

Chief Luther Standing Bear

Conversation

Conversation was never begun at once, nor in a hurried manner. No one was quick with a question, no matter how important, and no one was pressed for an answer. A pause giving time for thought was the truly courteous way of beginning and conducting a conversation. Silence was meaningful with the Lakota, and his granting a space of silence to the speech-maker and his own moment of silence before talking was done in the practice of true politeness and regard for the rule that 'thought comes before speech'.

Chief Luther Standing Bear

On Meditation

I am going to venture that the man who sat on the ground in his tipi meditating on life and its meaning, accepting the kinship of all creatures, and acknowledging unity with the universe of things was infusing into his being the true essence of civilization.

Chief Luther Standing Bear

We Do Not Want Riches

... I am poor and naked, but I am the chief of the
nation. We do not want riches but we do want to
train our children right. Riches would do us no good.
We could not take them with us to the other world.
We do not want riches. We want peace and love.

Chief Red Cloud (Makhpiya-luta), late 19th century

The Earth

The earth is your grandmother and mother, and she
is sacred. Every step that is taken upon her should be
as a prayer.

Black Elk (Hehaka Sapa)

[According to Black Elk, these words were spoke by
Ptesan Win, White Buffalo Calf Woman, when she brought
the scared pipe to the Sioux. In 1947–8, Black Elk passed
on his knowledge of the sacred rites of the Sioux to Joseph
Epes Brown. He died in 1950.]

You have noticed that everything an Indian does is in
a circle and that is because the Power of the Word
always works in circles, and everything tries to be

round. In the old days when we were a strong and happy people, all our power came to us from the scared hoop of the nation, and so long as the hoop was unbroken, the people flourished. The flowering tree was the living center of the hoop, and the circle of the four quarters nourished it. The east gave peace and light, the south gave warmth, the west gave rain, and the north with its cold and mighty wind gave strength and endurance. This knowledge came to us from the outer world with our religion. Everything the Power of the World does is done in a circle. The sky is round, and I have heard that the earth is round like a ball, and so are all the stars. The wind, in its greatest power, whirls. Birds make their nests in circles, for theirs is the same religion as ours. The sun comes forth and goes down again in a circle. The moon does the same, and both are round. Even the seasons form a great circle in their changing, and always come back again to where they were. The life of a man is a circle ... and so it is in everything where power moves. Our tepees were round like the nests of birds, and these were always set in a circle, the nation's hoop, a nest of many nests, where the Great Spirit meant for us to hatch our children.

Black Elk, 1931

The Life of an Indian

The life of an Indian is like the wings of the air. That is why you notice the hawk knows how to get his prey. The Indian is like that. The hawk swoops down on its prey; so does the Indian. In his lament he is like an animal. For instance, the coyote is sly; so is the Indian. The eagle is the same. That is why the Indian is always feathered up; he is a relative to the wings of the air.

Black Elk

… I hope the Great Heavenly Father, who will look down upon us, will give all the tribes His blessing, that we may go forth in peace, and live in peace all our days, and that He will look down upon our children and finally lift us far above this earth; and that our Heavenly Father will look upon our children as His children, that all the tribes may be His children, and as we shake hands today upon this broad plain, we may forever live in peace.

Chief Red Cloud

Closing Prayer

Creator, the evening sun sets on each
  one of us,

Our days draw to a sleepy close.

All the colours of the night sky beckon

And we follow on its brilliant yellow-red
  wing.

Creator, all those we have ever loved
  surround us,

We offer thanks and prayers for each one.

Blue, misty coloured memories of all the days

That we lived and laughed come to us at
  this hour.

Creator, we offer thanks for all your greatness

And for all the beauty and healing gifts of
  nature you have given us.

We say only one thing. We are all related.

From Mitakuye Oyasin ceremony

Every Step is a Prayer

One of our old, old holy men said, 'Every step you take upon the earth should be a prayer. The power of a pure and good soul is planted as a seed in every person's heart, and will grow as you walk in a sacred manner.' And if every step you take is a prayer, then you will always be walking in a sacred manner.

Charmaine White Face, 1993

The Great Mystery

From Wakan-Tanka, the Great Mystery, comes all power. It is from Wakan-Tanka that the holy man has wisdom and the power to heal and to make holy charms. Man knows that all healing plants are given by Wakan-Tanka; therefore they are holy. So too is the buffalo holy, because it is the gift of Wakan-Tanka.

Chief Flat-Iron (Maza Blaska), late 19th century

SNEHYTTENS

Delight in Nature

Isn't it lovely,

the little river cutting through
  the gorge

when you approach it slowly

while trout are standing

behind stones in the stream?

Isn't it lovely,

the river's thick grass banks?

But I shall never again

meet Willow Twig, my dear friend

I long to see again.

Well, that's how it is.

the winding run

of the stream through the gorge

is lovely.

Isn't it lovely,

the bluish rocky island out there

when you approach it slowly?

What does it matter

that the blowing spirits of the air

stray over the rocks

because the island is lovely

when you approach it

at an easy pace

and haul it in?

SUQUAMISH

When the last Red man shall have become a myth among the White Men, when your children's children find themselves alone in the field, the store, upon the highway, or in the pathless woods, they will not be all alone. In all the earth there is no place dedicated to Solitude. At night when the streets of your cities are silent and you think them deserted, they will throng with the returning hosts that once filled them and still fill this beloved land. The White man will never be alone. Let him be just and deal kindly with my people, for the dead are not powerless. Dead – I say? There is no death. Only a change of worlds.

Chief Seattle
From his speech to Isaac Stevens, Governor of
Washington Territory, 1854

How can you buy or sell the sky, the warmth of the land? The idea is strange to us … The rivers are our brothers, they quench our thirst. The rivers carry our canoes and feed our children … The air is precious to the red man, for all things share the same breath – the beast, the tree, the man, they all share the same breath.

This we know. The earth does not belong to man. Man belongs to the earth. This we know. All things are connected like the blood which unites one family. All things are connected.

Whatever befalls the earth, befalls the sons of the earth. Man did not weave the web of life; he is merely a strand in it. Whatever he does to the web, he does to himself.

…

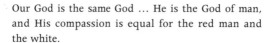

Our God is the same God ... He is the God of man, and His compassion is equal for the red man and the white.

...

Our religion is the traditions of our ancestors, the dreams of our old men, given them by the great Spirit, and the visions of our sachems, and is written in the hearts of our people.

Your dead cease to love you and the homes of their nativity as soon as they pass the portals of the tomb. They wander off beyond the stars, are soon forgotten and never return.

Our dead never forget the beautiful world that gave them being. They still love its winding rivers, its great mountains and its sequestered vales, and they ever yearn in tenderest affection over the lonely hearted living and often return to visit and comfort them.

...

It matters but little where we pass the remainder of our days. They are not many. The Indian's night promises to be dark. No bright star hovers about the horizon. Sad-voiced winds moan in the distance. Some grim Nemesis of our race is on the red man's trail, and wherever he goes he will still hear the sure approaching footsteps of the fell destroyer and prepare to meet his doom, as does the wounded doe that hears the approaching footsteps of the hunter.

A few more moons, a few winters and not one of all the mighty hosts that once filled this broad land or that now roam in fragmentary bands through these vast solitudes will remain to weep over the tombs of a people once as powerful and as hopeful as your own.

But why should we repine? Why should I murmur at the fate of my people? Tribes are made up of individuals and are no better than they. Men come and go like the waves of the sea. A tear, tamanamus, a dirge, and they are gone from our longing eyes forever. Even the white man, whose God walked and talked with him, as friend, is not exempt from the common destiny. We *may* be brothers after all. We shall see.

Chief Seattle, c.1880s

TEWA

Song of the Sky Loom

O our Mother the Earth, O our Father the Sky,

Your children are we, and with tired backs

We bring you the gifts you love.

Then weave for us a garment of brightness;

May the warp be the white light of morning,

May the weft be the red light of evening,

May the fringes be the falling rain,

May the border be the standing rainbow.

Thus weave for us a garment of brightness,

That we may walk fittingly where birds sing,

That we may walk fittingly where grass is
green,

O our Mother the Earth, O our Father the Sky.

From Herbert J. Spinden, *Songs of the Tewa*

Upward Going!

Yonder comes the dawn,

The universe grows green,

The road to the Underworld

Is open! Yet now we live,

Upward going, upward going!

[The Tewa Indians belong to a group of Tanoan tribes inhabiting the following pueblos: Nambé, San Ildefonso, San Juan, Santa Clara and Tesuque, all in New Mexico, and Hano in northeastern Arizona. The sky loom, as Dr Spinden points out, refers to the small desert rain, so characteristic of this part of the country.]

TLINGIT

Stop All This Idle Chatter

Stop all this idle chatter,

Let me hear no more gossip!

You drive me almost mad

With your idle and noisy chatter:

You old maids and old housewives,

Clean your fish, gather berries,

Mend your fires, boil the kettle;

Let me have peace and quiet!

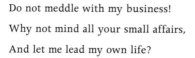

Do not meddle with my business!
Why not mind all your small affairs,
And let me lead my own life?

You old maids and you housewives,
Stop all this idle chatter,
Let me hear no more gossip,
Let me have peace and quiet!

I could tell tales if I wished to,
I too could tell tales and gossip,
I have an eye on you women!
I have seen things most curious.

Stop all this idle chatter,
Mend your fires, boil the kettle;
Let me have peace and quiet!

My heart is filled full of sorrow.
I only want my own sweetheart:

I cannot see her among you.

My own sweetheart, my beautiful.

Stop all this noisy chatter:

Mend your fires, boil your kettles,

Let me have peace and quiet!

Anon

WABANAKI

It is My Form and Person

It is my form and person that makes me great.

Hear the voice of my song – it is my voice.

I shield myself with secret coverings.

All your thoughts are known to me – blush!

I could draw you hence, were you a distant
island;

Though you were on the other hemisphere.

I speak to your naked heart.

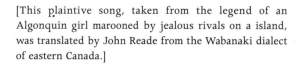

[This plaintive song, taken from the legend of an Algonquin girl marooned by jealous rivals on a island, was translated by John Reade from the Wabanaki dialect of eastern Canada.]

The Great Spirit

The Great Spirit is in all things; he is in the air we breathe. The Great Spirit is our Father, but the earth is our mother. She nourishes us; that which we put into the ground she returns to us ...

Big Thunder (Bedagi), late 19th century
Wabanaki Algonquin

WINNEBAGO

Long ago the language of the Winnebagos was different from what it is today, now the people no longer use such words in common speech. Indeed, no one knows the exact meaning of the wonderful words. The song is still used in some of the medicine ceremonies, but only the Medicine-Men, the Holy Men, understand its meaning. It is translated.

The medicine ceremony of the Winnebagos lasts

four days and nights. Holy songs are sung, and there is spoken ritual, when the Holy Man gives commandments and teaches the people the ways of goodness. Now and again, that the people may not become tired and drowsy, the ceremony is enlivened by dancing. So the slow part of this song is followed by a quick part which is the music of the dance. The medicine ceremony used to be very solemn and sacred in the olden times, and its mysteries were known only to the initiated. The white people called it the 'medicine religion' of the Winnebagos.

Holy Song

(Saith the Spirit,

'Dream, oh, dream again,

And tell of me,

Dream thou!')

Into solitude went I

And wisdom was revealed to me.

(Saith the Spirit,

'Dream, oh, dream again,

And tell of me,

Dream thou!')

Let the whole world hear me,

Wise am I!

    (Now saith the Spirit,

    'Tell of me,

        Dream thou!')

All was revealed to me;

From the beginning

Know I all, hear me!

All was revealed to me!

    (Now saith the Spirit,

    'Tell of me,

        Dream thou!')

Many Indian songs are sacred to certain occasions or ceremonies. Respect was always shown, therefore, for the natural and sometimes superstitious reluctance of the people to sing such songs at other than the proper time, or even to consent to the recording of them. When a singer chose such a song for his contribution, it was well, indeed; but no one was ever urged to desecrate anything held sacred, no matter what the motive.

From Alice C. Fletcher, *The Indians' Book*

This Newly Created World

Pleasant it looked,

this newly created world.

Along the entire length and breadth

of the earth, our grandmother,

extended the green reflection

of her covering

and the escaping odors

were pleasant to inhale.

Prayer

Earthmaker, our father, listen to me. On earth, most pitiable is the life we lead. Falling and dying, we stumble along the road. True it is that you told us what to do so that we might obtain the goods and benefits of life. That we are aware of. To achieve the good life as you ordained, this, too, we know and we shall attempt. We shall indeed attempt to secure light and life. But do you, nevertheless, cause real life to appear among us? This is what we ask of you in all humility.

YUMA

Curing Song

Your heart is good.

[The Spirit]) Shining Darkness will be here.

You think only of sad unpleasant things,

You are to think of goodness.

Lie down and sleep here.

Shining darkness will join us.

You think of this goodness in your dream.

Goodness will be given to you,

I will speak for it, and it will come to pass.

It will happen here,

I will ask for your good,

It will happen as I sit by you,

It will be done as I sit here in this place.

From C. Daryll Forde,
Ethnography of the Yuma Indians

ZUÑI

Prayer at Sunrise

Now this day,

My sun father,

Now that you have come out standing
to your sacred place,

That from which we draw the water of
life,

Prayer meal,

Here I give to you.

Your long life,

Your old age,

Your waters,

Your seeds,

Your riches

Your power,

Your strong spirit,

All these to me may you grant.

Sun Rays

See!

there across the sky

the Drawers-of-straight-Lines

flash their furrows of fire.

It is the Mind of the Father

on the borderland of Time,

the Father,

yearning,

yearning for his children

turned from the sky.

Adapted by Ina Sizer Cassidy

Prayer to a Dead Wife

Even so may it be.

Now this day,

My ancestors,

You have attained the far-off place of
    waters [land of the dead].

This day,

Carrying plume wands,

Plume wands which I have prepared for
    your use,

I pass you on your roads.

Beseeching the Breath

Beseeching the breath of the
    divine one,

His life-giving breath,

His breath of old age,

His breath of waters,

His breath of seeds,

His breath of riches,

His breath of fecundity,

His breath of power,

His breath of strong spirit,

His breath of all good fortune
    whatsoever,

Asking for his breath

And into my warm body drawing his
    breath,

I add to your breath

That happily you may always live.

Anon

They Went to the Moon Mother

The two stars are saying this

to all the scared bundles here:

'Rejoice! Holy bundles, sacred bundles,
    because of your wise thoughts your Moon
    Mother spoke, gave her word.

Rejoice! You will be granted many blessings,
    flowing silt.'

Maskers, rainmakers

soaking the earth with rain,

making lightning, stretching, stretching.

I, the masker, say this to you;
'By the Moon Mother's word
from the Middle Place all the way to Dawn Lake
your paths will be complete,
you will reach old age.'

From Barbara Tedlock,
Songs of the Zuni Kachina Society

The Sunrise Call

Rise! arise! arise!

Rise! arise, arise!

Wake ye! arise, life is greeting thee.

Wake ye, arise, ever watchful be.

Mother Life-god, she is calling thee!

Mother Life-god, she is calling thee!

Mother Life-god, she is greeting thee.

All arise, arise, arise!

Rise! arise! arise!

Mighty Sun-god! Give thy light to us,

Let it guide us, let it aid us.

See it rise! See it rise!

How the heart glows, how the soul
  delights,

On the music of the sunlight.

Watch it rise! Watch it rise!

Wake ye! arise, life is greeting thee.

Wake ye, arise, ever watchful be.

Mother Life-god, she is calling thee!

Mother Life-god, she is greeting thee.

All arise, arise, arise!

Rise! arise! arise!

Invocation to the Sun-God

Grant, O Sun-god, thy protection!

Guard this helpless infant sleeping.

Grant, O Sun-god, thy protection!

Guard this helpless infant sleeping,

Resting peaceful, resting peaceful.

Starry guardians forever joyful,

Faithful Moon-god forever watchful.

Grant, O Sun-god, thy protection!

Guard this helpless infant sleeping.

Spirit living, Spirit resting,

Guard us, lead us, aid us, love us.

Sun-god forever, Spirit living, Spirit resting,

Guard us, lead us, aid us, love us.

Sun-god forever.

EPILOGUE

TRIBUTES

The American Indian

Ye say they all have passed away,
  That noble race and brave,
That their light canoes have vanished
  From off the crested wave;
That 'mid the forest where they roamed
  There rings no hunter's shout,
But their name is on your waters;
Ye may not wash it out.

Ye say their conelike cabins
  That clustered o'er the vale
Have fled away like withered leaves

Before the autumn gale.

But their memory liveth on your hills,

Their baptism on your shore;

Your everlasting rivers speak

   Their dialect of yore.

Ye say no lover wooes his maid,

   No warrior leads his band,

All in forgotten graves are laid,

E'en great chiefs of the clan;

That where their council fires were lit

   The shepherd tends his flock,

But their names are on your mountains

   And survive the earthquake shock.

Mrs Sigourney and H.B. Wood

I speak for each no-tongued tree

That, spring by spring, doth nobler be,

And dumbly and most wistfully

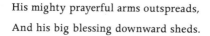

His mighty prayerful arms outspreads,
And his big blessing downward sheds.

Sidney Lanier

But there's a dome of nobler span,
   A temple given
Thy faith, that bigots dare not ban –
   Its space is heaven!
Its roof star-pictured Nature's ceiling,
Where, trancing the rapt spirit's feeling.
And God Himself to man revealing,
   Th' harmonious spheres
Make music, though unheard their pealing
By mortal ears!

Thomas Campbell

God! Sing ye meadow streams with gladsome
  voice!

Ye pine-groves, with your soft and soul-like
  sounds!

Ye eagles, playmates of the mountain storm!

Ye lightnings, the dread arrows of the clouds!

Ye signs and wonders of the elements,

Utter forth God, and fill the hills with praise!

Earth, with her thousand voices, praises God!

Samuel Taylor Coleridge

Prophetic of the coming joy and strife,

  Like the wild western war-chief sinking

  Calm to the end he eyes unblinking,

Earth's voice is jubilant in ebbing life.

He for his happy hunting-fields,

  Forgets the droning chant, and yields

  His numbered breaths to exultation

  In the proud anticipation:

Shouting the glories of his nation,

Shouting the grandeur of his race.

Shouting his own great deeds of daring:

And when at last death grasps his face,

And stiffened on the ground in peace

He lies with all his painted terrors glaring;

Hushed are the tribe to hear a threading cry:

Not from the dead man;

Not from the standers-by:

The spirit of the red man

Is welcomed by his fathers up on high.

From George Meredith,
'Ode to the Spirit of Earth in Autumn'

ACKNOWLEDGEMENTS

Thanks to Dr Mick Gidley, for kindly agreeing to write the Introduction and for his editorial assistance, and to Dr Dorian Hayes, Curator of the North American literature collection of the British Library, for his advice and assistance in the research.

The author and publishers wish to thank the University of Nebraska Press for granting permission to reprint extracts of poems from *The Sky Clears: Poetry of the American Indians* by A. Grove Day, and the extract from *Speaking of Indians* by Ella Deloria. Thanks also to Charmaine White Face for 'Every Step is a Prayer'.

Every effort has been made to secure permission to reproduce other material protected by copyright. The author and publishers will be pleased to make good any omissions brought to their attention in future printings of this book.